EF

n.g.

VOX LATINA

VOX LATINA

A GUIDE TO
THE PRONUNCIATION OF
CLASSICAL LATIN

BY

W. SIDNEY ALLEN

Professor of Comparative Philology in the
University of Cambridge

CAMBRIDGE
AT THE UNIVERSITY PRESS
1965

PUBLISHED BY
THE SYNDICS OF THE CAMBRIDGE UNIVERSITY PRESS

Bentley House, 200 Euston Road, London, N.W. 1
American Branch: 32 East 57th Street, New York, N.Y. 10022
West African Office: P.O. Box 33, Ibadan, Nigeria

©

CAMBRIDGE UNIVERSITY PRESS

1965

LIBRARY OF CONGRESS CATALOGUE
CARD NUMBER: 65-16204

Printed in Great Britain at the University Printing House, Cambridge
(Brooke Crutchley, University Printer)

FOREWORD

In discussions on the subject of Latin pronunciation two questions are commonly encountered; they tend to be of a rhetorical nature, and are not entirely confined to non-classical disputants. First, why should we concern ourselves with the pronunciation of a dead language? And second, how in any case can we know how the language was originally pronounced?

In answer to the first question, it may reasonably be held that it is desirable to seek an appreciation of Latin literature, and that such literature was based on a living language. Moreover, much of early literature, and poetry in particular, was orally composed and was intended to be spoken and heard rather than written and seen. If, therefore, we are to try and appreciate an author's full intentions, including the phonetic texture of his work, we must put ourselves as nearly as possible in the position of the native speaker and hearer of his day. Otherwise, however full our grammatical and lexical understanding of the work, we shall still be missing an important element of the contemporary experience. It is true that we can have a lively appreciation of, say, Shakespeare, whilst reading or hearing his work in a modern pronunciation—but in this case the two languages are not far removed from one another, and whilst individual sounds may have changed to some extent, the relations between them have been largely preserved; the situation is already very different, even within English, if we go back only as far as Chaucer. It is said that Burke used to read French poetry as if it were English; when one considers the vowel harmonies of a line like Hugo's 'Un frais parfum sortait des touffes d'asphodèle', one can only conclude that his appreciation must have been minimal!

We are here concerned primarily to reconstruct the educated

pronunciation of Rome in the Golden Age. But it will be necessary to take note of certain variations even within this period, and of interest in some cases to refer to features of more colloquial speech, and of preceding or following periods.

The degree of accuracy with which we can reconstruct the ancient pronunciation varies from sound to sound, but for the most part can be determined within quite narrow limits. In some favourable cases it is possible to reconstruct such niceties of pronunciation as it would be unreasonable to demand in normal reading; and the present book is not so unpractical as to suggest that more than a reasonable approximation should then be made. But the knowledge should nevertheless be available to the reader, so that, whatever pronunciation he in fact adopts, he may know to what degree and in what respects it differs from the probable original. For many of us, already well set in our ways, it will inevitably continue to be a case of 'uideo meliora proboque; deteriora sequor'; but scholarship surely requires that we should at least know what is known or at any rate probable.

It is claims such as those of the preceding paragraph that commonly evoke the second question 'How do we know?' And there is no one simple answer to it. The kinds of evidence and argument are various, and will become familiar in the course of the pages that follow; but the principal types of data invoked in phonetic reconstruction may be summarized as follows: (1) specific statements of Latin grammarians and other authors regarding the pronunciation of the language; (2) puns, plays on words, ancient etymologies, and imitations of natural sounds; (3) the representation of Latin words in other languages; (4) developments in the Romance languages; (5) the spelling conventions of Latin, and particularly scribal or epigraphic variations; and (6) the internal structure of the Latin language itself, including its metrical patterns. Our arguments will seldom rely on one type of evidence alone, and the combinations of evidence will vary from case to case. The grammarians are mostly of very late date, but their evidence is important as confirming the continuation of features established for earlier periods by other means; frequently also they quote the views or practice of earlier writers; and it is a characteristic of their profession to preserve earlier traditions long after they have vanished from normal speech.

In view of the prevalence of the second question, it is at least as important that the reader should be equipped with reasons as with results; and particular attention has been paid to setting out 'how we know what we know' in language that is, so far as possible, free from technical complications. In the process of reconstruction we are of course dependent on a variety of linguistic theories and techniques, but since the present book is not directed primarily to the linguistic specialist, no technical terms have been used without due explanation.[1] References to the specialist literature have also been kept to a minimum; this must not, however, be taken to minimize the debt that is owed to a large number of books and articles, on every aspect of the subject, over a period of roughly a century; and in particular to such eminent overall studies as Seelmann's *Die Aussprache des Latein nach physiologisch-historischen Grundsätzen* (1885), Sommer's *Handbuch der lateinischen Laut- und Formenlehre* (1914), and Sturtevant's *The Pronunciation of Greek and Latin* (1940). Two particularly useful recent works may also be specially mentioned: Maria Bonioli's *La pronuncia del latino nelle scuole dall'antichità al rinascimento*, Parte 1 (Torino, 1962), and Alfonso Traina's *L'alfabeto e la pronunzia del latino* (2nd edn., Bologna, 1963).

My thanks are due to several colleagues and students for encouragement and suggestions in the preparation of this work; in particular to Mr A. G. Hunt, of the Department of Education, University of Cambridge; and to Mr W. B. Thompson, of the Department of Education, University of Leeds, who 'tried

---

[1] The more common phonetic terms are introduced and explained in a preliminary chapter, and an asterisk against the first occurrence of a term in the text indicates that it is there discussed.

out' an early draft on a number of classical school-teachers and gave me the benefit of their comments and criticisms. I am also grateful for the interest expressed by the Joint Association of Classical Teachers, and by the Education Subcommittee of the Council of the Classical Association. Lastly, I owe a special debt to Mr R. G. G. Coleman, of Emmanuel College, Cambridge, who read the whole of the final draft and made a number of valuable comments and suggestions.

W. S. A.

CAMBRIDGE
March 1964

CONTENTS

Video rem operosiorem esse quam putaram,
emendate pronuntiare.

(LEO, in D. Erasmi *De recta Latini Graecique sermonis pronuntiatione Dialogo*)

PHONETIC INTRODUCTION

(i) Syllable, vowel and consonant

In any continuous piece of utterance we may perceive certain variations of prominence, characterizing its constituent sounds in such a way that the more prominent alternate with the less prominent in a more or less regular succession. A diagrammatic representation of the opening of the *Aeneid*, for example, would appear somewhat as follows in terms of relative prominence:

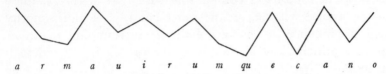

It will be seen that the heights of the 'peaks' and the depths of the 'valleys' are various; but it is their relative and not their absolute measurement that is important from the standpoint of linguistic structure (omitted for present purposes is the heightening of certain peaks as a consequence of stress or intonation). In the above example there appear seven peaks, with six valleys between them, thus:

$$\text{peaks} \quad a - a - i - u - e - a - o$$
$$\text{valleys} \quad m - u - r - qu - c - n$$

The number of SYLLABLES in a piece generally corresponds to the number of peaks of prominence. The sounds which habitually occur at these peaks we term VOWELS, and those which occur in the valleys CONSONANTS.

The classification is not, however, entirely straightforward. Thus the *r* of *uirum* is in the valley, but that of *arma* is on the slope; the point here is that in *uirum* the *r* is less prominent than both the preceding *i* and the following *u*, whereas the *r* in *arma*, whilst less prominent than the preceding *a*, is more prominent than the following *m*. Similar considerations apply to the *m*'s of *arma* and of *uirumque*. At this point it will be advisable to consider the nature of the so far undefined 'prominence'. In Daniel Jones' words, 'The prominence of sounds may be due to inherent sonority (carrying power), to length or to stress or to special intonation, or to combinations of these'; so far as concerns the vowel/consonant distinction, inherent sonority is the most generally relevant factor—but there are exceptions. Thus the initial *u* of *uirum* lies in a valley, whereas the *u* of the second syllable forms a peak; yet the articulation of both by the tongue and lips is more or less identical. Here the point is that in its position before *i* the initial *u* is reduced to a very short duration,[1] with consequent loss of prominence (although its inherent sonority is comparable with that of the *i*); the *u* of the second syllable, on the other hand, is of high sonority and prominence in contrast with the surrounding *r* and *m*. Similar principles would apply to the two *i*'s in a word such as *iussit*.

Sounds which may function either as peaks or as valleys of prominence, whilst classified as vowels in their peak (or 'nuclear') function, are generally termed SEMIVOWELS, and classed with the consonants, in their valley (or 'marginal') function. Thus Latin *i* and *u* may represent both vowels and consonants, and Latin does not distinguish the two functions in writing—unlike e.g. English, which distinguishes *i* and *u* from *y* and *w*.

Finally, it may be noted that two vowels can follow one another as independent peaks, by means of some diminution of energy between them: thus e.g. Latin *a-it, faci-at, abi-it, mortu-us, medi-us, tenu-is*.

(ii) Consonants

A primary classification of consonants is into the categories of VOICED and VOICELESS. Voiced sounds involve an approximation of the two edges of the vocal cords, so that when air passes through them it sets up a characteristic vibration, known technically as 'glottal tone' or VOICE; voiceless sounds involve a

---

[1] Probably also with some relaxation of lip-rounding.

clear separation of the cords, so that no such vibration occurs. The difference may be exemplified by the English (voiced) *z* and (voiceless) *s*. If the ears are closed, the vibration of the former can be clearly heard by the speaker; the vibration can also be felt by placing a finger on the protuberance of the thyroid cartilage ('Adam's apple').

Sounds may be further classified according to the position or organ involved in their articulation. Thus LABIAL (or BI-LABIAL) involves the articulation of the two lips (e.g. English *p*), LABIO-DENTAL the articulation of the upper teeth and lower lip (e.g. English *f*), DENTAL the articulation of the tongue-tip and upper teeth (e.g. English *th*), ALVEOLAR the articulation of the tongue-tip and upper gums (e.g. English *t*), VELAR the articulation of the back of the tongue and the back of the palate (e.g. English *k*).

If the tongue or lips form a complete closure, during which air is prevented from passing through the mouth until the closure is released, the resulting sound is termed a STOP. Stops are further subdivided into PLOSIVES and NASALS according to whether the nasal passages are closed or open during the articulation of the stop; thus English has the plosives *p*, *b* (bilabial, voiceless and voiced), *t*, *d* (alveolar), *k*, *g* (velar), and the nasals *m* (bilabial), *n* (alveolar), and as *ng* in *sing* (velar). In most languages the nasals are all inherently voiced.

The 'plosion' of the plosives refers to the effect which is produced when the oral closure is released. If the vocal cords are left open for a brief period after the plosion, producing an audible type of '*h*-sound', the consonant is termed ASPIRATED —there is clear aspiration, for example, of voiceless plosives at the beginning of words in English and German. In French, on the other hand, the vocal cords are closed almost simultaneously with the oral plosion, and the result is a relatively UNASPIRATED sound.

If the articulating organs are not completely closed, but if the channel between them is so narrow as to cause an audible effect as the air passes through it, the resulting sound is termed a FRICATIVE. English examples are *f* and *v* (labio-dental,

3

voiceless and voiced), and *s* and *z* (alveolar). The ASPIRATE, *h*, is also sometimes called a 'glottal fricative'.

If one side of the tongue forms a closure, but the other side permits air to flow freely,[1] the result is a LATERAL consonant, such as the English *l*. Such sounds are sometimes classed with the *r*-sounds as 'liquids' (see p. 32).

(iii) Vowels

Variations of vowel quality are effected primarily by the raising of different portions of the tongue's surface towards the palate, and by different degrees of such raising resulting in different degrees of aperture between tongue and palate. Vowels may thus be classified according to (*a*) how far FRONT or BACK they are articulated (i.e. involving more forward or more backward areas of the tongue and palate), and (*b*) how CLOSE or OPEN they are (i.e. involving greater or lesser raising of the tongue).

The relations of the vowels to one another may then be conveniently represented in terms of a two-dimensional diagram. When so represented they tend to fall into a triangular or quadrilateral pattern,[2] such as:

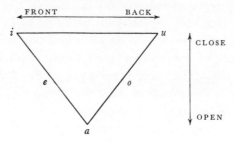

Vowels intermediate between front and back are referred to as CENTRAL, and vowels intermediate between close and open as MID (the so-called 'neutral' vowel of standard southern British English, as at the end of *sofa* or *finger*, is a mid-central vowel).

---

[1] Alternatively there may be a central closure, with air-flow on both sides.
[2] It should be mentioned that such a pattern applies more exactly to the acoustic effects of the vowels than to their actual physiological articulation.

Associated with the features already mentioned are various degrees of lip-ROUNDING; generally speaking back vowels are associated with rounding and front vowels with its absence (lip-spreading). Thus the English *u* and *i*, in e.g. *put*, *pit*, are respectively close back rounded and close front unrounded. Sometimes, however, rounding is associated with a front vowel and spreading with a back vowel—thus the French *u*, German *ü*, and classical Greek ʋ are front rounded vowels, and back unrounded vowels occur in some languages.

Vowels are normally articulated with the nasal passages closed (by raising the soft palate or 'velum'), but if the nasal passages are left open the result is a NASALIZED vowel (as e.g. in French *on*, phonetically transcribed [õ]).

DIPHTHONGS are formed by articulating a vowel and then, within the same syllable, making a gradual change of articulation (or 'glide') in the direction of another vowel. Most commonly, but not inevitably, the first element of a diphthong is more open than the second. Thus the diphthong of English *high* involves a glide from *a* towards *i*, of *how* from *a* towards *u*, and of *hay* from *e* towards *i*.

In many languages vowels fall into two degrees of LENGTH, LONG and SHORT. By and large the difference corresponds to a greater as opposed to a lesser duration—but not invariably so. Other features, such as muscular tension, difference of quality, and tendency to diphthongization, may be at least as important (they are, for example, in distinguishing the so-called 'short' vowel of English *bit* from the so-called 'long' vowel of *beat*).

(iv) Accent

ACCENT is a general term covering two distinct linguistic functions, and two different modes of implementing these functions. The two functions of accent are termed 'delimitative' and 'culminative'. The first of these, as its name suggests, concerns the fact that in certain languages there are restrictions on the position of the accent within the word such that, given this position, it is possible to infer from it the boundaries of words.

Thus in Czech or Hungarian, words are normally accented by stress on their first syllable; the occurrence of stress in these languages thus indicates the beginning of a word. In Armenian, words are normally stressed on their final syllable, so that the occurrence of stress here indicates the end of a word. In Polish, words are normally stressed on their penultimate syllable, so that the occurrence of stress indicates a word-boundary after the next syllable. The accent of classical Latin is delimitative in a rather complex manner (see p. 83), but that of the majority of Greek dialects only trivially so. In English or Russian, for example, where the accent is free (cf. English *ímport, impórt*; Russian *múka* 'torment', *muká* 'flour'), the accent is of course not delimitative, since it is impossible to predict word-boundaries from it. In such cases the accent has only its 'culminative' function of indicating the number of full words in the utterance[1] (a function that is also included in the delimitative accent); the culminative function may in fact be considered as a phonetic expression of the individuality of the word, focused upon a particular portion of it.

Whether delimitative or merely culminative in function, two specific modes of accentuation must be recognized, (*a*) PITCH, or TONAL accent, and (*b*) STRESS, or DYNAMIC accent. The tonal accent involves a raising of the voice-pitch at a particular point, and the dynamic accent involves an increase in the muscular effort (primarily by the abdominal muscles).

It is important to distinguish tone from INTONATION. The former refers to the pitch-patterns operative within individual words, whereas 'intonation' refers to the pitch-pattern operative over the whole clause or sentence. There may of course be, and there usually is, considerable interaction between these two patterns; thus the pitch-pattern of a given word may vary greatly in accordance with the pitch-pattern of the sentence; such an effect is sometimes referred to as a 'perturbation' of the word-tones. Rather similar considerations apply in the case of stress, though one might expect the 'perturbation' to be less in

---

[1] Since it is free, however, it is capable, unlike the delimitative accent, of carrying differences of meaning (as in the English and Russian examples cited).

those languages where the word-stress is strong, as, for example, in English; even here, however, some variation is possible, as for instance in the word *fundamental* in the two sentences *it's quíte fundaméntal* and *it's a fúndamental prínciple*. In French, stress is a feature of the word only as an isolate (in which case it falls on the final syllable); in connected speech, however, it is rather a feature of the sense-group.

Naturally the syllables in a word have varying degrees of stress, but by *the* stressed syllable we mean the syllable which carries the *main* stress.

Ceteris paribus, stressed sounds produce greater intensity of air-pressure and are perceived as louder than others; but, as already mentioned, the overall prominence of a sound depends upon other features also, such as inherent sonority, duration and intonation; and it is not always easy to disentangle the various causes contributing to its perception.

The distribution of accentual types amongst the languages of the world is a matter for observation rather than prediction. Some more or less universal rules do, however, seem to be emerging. For example, it has been claimed that if a language has significant distinctions of vowel-length, as Latin or Greek, it will not generally have a free dynamic accent; and if a language requires an analysis of its syllabic peaks into '*morae*' (as classical Greek), its accent is likely to be tonal, but if (as in Latin) no such analysis is demanded, the accent is likely to be dynamic.

(v) Speech and writing

In the study of a 'dead' language there is inevitably a main emphasis on the written word. But it is well to remember that writing is secondary to speech, and however much it may deviate from it, has speech as its ultimate basis. The written symbols correspond, in a more or less complete manner, to phonological or grammatical elements of speech; and, as Martinet points out, 'vocal quality is directly responsible for the linearity of speech and the consequent linearity of script'. It is therefore in a sense misleading to speak of written symbols as being pronounced—rather is it the other way round, the symbols represent spoken elements. But when, as in the case of Latin today, most utterance consists of reading from a written text, the traditional terminology of 'pronouncing letters' may reasonably be tolerated, and is in fact maintained in this book.

In Latin, as in modern European languages, the correspondence is between symbols (letters) and phonological elements, and is much more regular than in some languages, such as English or French or Modern Greek, which notoriously use different symbols or combinations of symbols to indicate the same sound.

It is sometimes stated that an ideal writing-system would have a symbol for every sound—that it would in fact be a kind of 'visible speech'. Since, however, the number of sounds in a language is infinite, and the 'same' sound probably never precisely recurs, this requirement is quite impracticable. It is also unnecessary, as alphabets from earliest times have recognized. The number of symbols can be reduced to manageable proportions without any resultant ambiguity by a process which has long been unconsciously followed, and the theoretical basis of which has been worked out in recent years.

What is required is not one symbol per sound, but one symbol per PHONEME. A 'phoneme' is a class of similar sounds that are *significantly* different from other sounds, e.g. the class of *t*-sounds in English *tin*, *hat*, etc., or the class of *d*-sounds in *din*, *had*, etc. The (voiceless) *t*-phoneme and the (voiced) *d*-phoneme are different phonemes in English, and so require distinct symbols, because *tin* has a different meaning from *din*, *hat* has a different meaning from *had*, etc.; in technical terminology, the members of the *t* and *d* phonemes are in 'parallel distribution', i.e. they can contrast significantly with one another, and with members of other phonemes, in otherwise identical immediate environments ((-)*in*, *ha*(-), etc.).

On the other hand, the fact that an initial *t* in English (as in *tin*) is more strongly aspirated than a final *t* (as in *hat*) is not responsible for any difference of meaning, since the two varieties occur only in different environments, and so cannot contrast

8

with one another—they are in 'complementary' and not parallel distribution. They are thus both members (or 'allophones') of the same *t*-phoneme; only one symbol is required to write them, since the difference in sound is predictable from their environment, i.e. initial or final position as the case may be. It should be noted, however, that the phonemic distribution of sounds varies from language to language; in a language such as classical Greek or modern Hindi, for example, aspirated and unaspirated *t*-sounds belong to separate phonemes, since the occurrence of one or the other is not predictable from environment and they may contrast significantly (e.g. Greek τείνω 'stretch', θείνω 'strike'; Hindi *sāt* 'seven', *sāth* 'with').

The number of phonemes in a language varies; the number of consonants, for example, varies from 8 in Hawaiian, through 24 in English and 32 in Sanskrit, to 80 in the Caucasian Ubykh. Latin, according to the analysis adopted,[1] has from 15 to 18 consonant phonemes in native words.

This 'phonemic' principle, then, is an economic principle, ensuring that the minimal number of symbols are used consistent with unambiguous representation of speech. And Latin spelling comes very near to being completely phonemic. The principal shortcoming in this respect concerns the vowels, since no distinction is made in standard orthography between short and long—thus, for example, *malus* 'bad' and *uictum* (from *uinco*) are not distinguished from *malus* 'apple-tree' and *uictum* (from *uiuo*); also no distinction is made between consonantal and vocalic *i* and *u*, as in *adiecit, adiens* and *inuitus, minuit*, etc. (*uoluit* provides a case of actual ambiguity).

When indicating particular sounds in a phonetic notation it is customary to enclose the symbols in square brackets, e.g. [tʰ] to represent the initial sound of English *tin*; phonemic symbols, on the other hand, are conventionally set between obliques, e.g. /t/ for the phoneme which includes the initial sound of *tin* and the final sound of *hat*. In a book intended primarily for the

---

[1] Depending upon whether the [ŋ] sounds of *magnus, incipio*, etc. (see pp. 23, 27) are classed together as a separate phoneme, and whether *qu, gu* are treated as single phonemes (though represented by digraphs) or as sequences of *c, g* and consonantal *u* (see pp. 16, 25).

classical and general reader rather than the technical linguist and phonetician it has seemed desirable to keep phonetic symbols to a minimum. This inevitably involves some theoretical mixing of phonetic, phonemic, and graphic levels of statement, but no practical confusion should thereby be caused. A rigorous separation of levels (as is necessary on e.g. pp. 15, 28) would lead to greater complexity of statement, which would tend to obscure the primary purpose of this study. For the same reason the conventions of the International Phonetic Alphabet have in some cases been modified in the direction of more familiar forms—e.g. by the use of [y] instead of [j] for the palatal semivowel (where the latter could be misleading to the general English reader), and by the use of the macron instead of the colon for vowel length.

Note: Where English equivalents are given for Latin sounds, the reference, unless otherwise stated, is to the standard or 'Received Pronunciation' (R.P.) of southern British English. The choice of this form of English as a basis of comparison is made on purely practical grounds. It is impossible to cite examples that will be equally applicable to all nationalities and dialects of English, and one must perforce select a standard; and 'R.P.' is by far the best documented and familiar of such standards. Nevertheless, care has been taken to select examples which, so far as possible, will not be positively misleading to speakers of other forms of English.

CHAPTER I

CONSONANTS

Before considering the individual sounds in detail, it is important to note that wherever a *double* consonant is written in Latin it stands for a correspondingly lengthened sound. This is clearly seen from its effect on the quantity of a preceding syllable, the first syllable of e.g. *accidit* or *ille* always being 'heavy' (see p. 89) although the vowel is short. Quite apart from metrical considerations, it is necessary to observe this in pronunciation, since otherwise no distinction will be made between such pairs as *ager* and *agger*, *anus* and *annus*. English speakers need to pay special attention to this point, since double consonants are so pronounced in English only where they belong to separate elements of a compound word—as in *rat-tail, hop-pole, bus-service, unnamed,* etc.; otherwise the written double consonants of English (e.g. in *bitter, happy, running*) have the function only of indicating that the preceding vowel is short. The English compounds in fact provide a useful model for the correct pronunciation of the Latin double (or 'long') consonants.

In early systems of Latin spelling, double consonants were written single; the double writing does not appear in inscriptions until the beginning of the second century B.C. Ennius is said to have introduced the new spelling (cf. Festus, under *soli-taurilia*), but in an inscription of 117 B.C. the old spelling is still more common than the new.[1] The single spelling in such cases does not of course indicate single pronunciation, any more than the normal single writing of long vowels indicates a short pronunciation.

---

[1] Another device, mentioned by the grammarians and occasionally found in Augustan inscriptions, is to place the sign '*sicilicum*' over the letter to indicate doubling (in the manner of the Arabic 'shadda')—thus, for example, oṡA=*ossa*.

(i) Voiceless* plosives*[1]

There are four varieties of these in Latin—bilabial*, dental*, velar*, and labio-velar (see p. 16); they are written as *p*, *t*, *c*, and *qu* respectively. The first three have a close affinity to the sounds represented by English *p*, *t*, *k* (or 'hard' *c*).

The English voiceless plosives, particularly at the beginning of a word, are clearly aspirated*. The corresponding Latin sounds were relatively unaspirated, as is shown by the fact that they were generally transcribed as π, τ, κ respectively in Greek (e.g. Καπετωλιον, Κοιντος for *Capitolium*, *Quintus*); for the Greek letters can only stand for unaspirated plosives. The Romance languages also generally agree in lacking aspiration (e.g. the pronunciation of Spanish *tiempo*, from Latin *tempus*).

But since, as in English and unlike Greek, there was no contrast in native Latin words between unaspirated and aspirated plosives, and so no possibility of significant confusion, some degree of aspiration could theoretically have been tolerated; and one piece of evidence, though indirect, is rather suggestive in this connexion.

When an English speaker listens to an Indian language such as Hindi (which, like ancient Greek, distinguishes between aspirated and unaspirated consonants), he tends to interpret the unaspirated voiceless plosives, particularly at the beginning of a word, as if they were voiced* (hearing *p* as *b*, *k* as *g*, etc.). The reason is that, since voicelessness in English is normally associated with aspiration, complete absence of aspiration, as in Hindi *p*, *t*, *k*, etc., is heard as voice*, for, without special training, we inevitably listen to a foreign language in terms of our native system of phonemes. Now there are some Greek words containing initial voiceless unaspirated consonants which are borrowed into Latin with *voiced* consonants; thus κυβερνῶ becomes *guberno*, πύξος becomes *buxus*, κόμμι becomes *gummi*, κράβ(β)ατος becomes *grab(b)atus*, and so on; which could mean that in this respect the Roman listening to Greek was in much

---

[1] An asterisk after a term indicates that it is explained in the phonetic introduction.

the same situation as the Englishman listening to Hindi, i.e. that the voiceless plosives of his own language, at least in initial position, tended to be aspirated.[1] A number of the words so borrowed appear to have been of a colloquial character, and they may be further augmented from Vulgar Latin, as e.g. (reconstructed) *botteca* from ἀποθήκη (cf. Italian *bottega*), or (*Appendix Probi*, K. iv, 199)[2] *blasta* from πλαστ-. That the tendency was also prevalent in earlier times is evident from Cicero's statement (*Or.* 160) that Ennius used always to say '*Burrus*' for *Pyrrhus*. In fact the phenomenon seems to be particularly associated with non-classical borrowings, in which the actual speech is likely to be reflected rather than a literary consciousness of the Greek spelling.[3]

It is admittedly a minor detail that is in question; but the discussion will have served to show how light may sometimes be shed on ancient linguistic problems by the observation of modern parallels; and on a more practical level, that one should probably not insist too strongly on the complete avoidance of aspiration in Latin.

t It is sometimes said that the Latin sound represented by this letter differed from the comparable sound in English, since the latter does not have a dental* but an alveolar* articulation (in which the tongue makes contact with the gum-ridge behind the upper teeth rather than with the teeth themselves); whereas Latin, to judge from the evidence of the Romance languages, had a true dental articulation (as, for example, in French). It should, however, be mentioned that the grammarians do appear to prescribe something not unlike the English alveolar contact, in contrast with a pure dental contact for the voiced sound of *d* (e.g. † Terentianus Maurus, K. vi, 331).[4] It would be unwise

---

[1] Though presumably less so than those which later came to be written as such (see p. 26).

[2] This and similar references are to the volumes of Keil's *Grammatici Latini*.

[3] It has been pointed out that many of the words in question are probably non-Indo-European, and borrowed by both Greek and Latin independently from some 'Mediterranean' source. But this does not invalidate the argument, since the different forms in which they were borrowed indicate a different interpretation of the sounds by Greek and Latin speakers.

[4] Texts of references marked thus (†) are given in Appendix A (1).

to make too much of this evidence; for the Greek and Latin grammarians never succeeded in discovering the general distinction between voice and voicelessness,[1] and so were quite liable to seize on any minor, or even imaginary, difference of articulation in order to distinguish between a particular pair of sounds (cf. p. 21). But at the same time the existence of such statements once again makes it questionable whether one should insist on suppressing English speech-habits in this particular connexion.

c   Latin *c* in all cases represents a *velar* plosive*—i.e., in popular terminology, it is always 'hard' and never 'soft'—even before the front* vowels *e* and *i*. Inscriptions in fact sometimes write *k* for *c* in this environment (e.g. *pake*), and Greek regularly transcribes Latin *c* by κ (e.g. κηνσωρ, Κικερων for *cēnsor, Cicero*); the sound was also preserved in words borrowed from Latin by Celtic and Germanic between the first and fifth centuries A.D. In the grammarians there is no suggestion of anything other than a velar plosive; and Varro (Priscian, K. ii, 30) provides positive evidence by citing *anceps* beside *ancora* as an example of the velar value of *n* (see p. 27)—which only makes sense if the following sound is the same in both cases. There is a further hint in the alliterative formula '*censuit consensit consciuit*' (Livy, i, 32, 13).

It is true that in the course of time a 'softening' took place before *e* and *i* (compare the pronunciation of *c* in French *cent*, Italian *cento*, Spanish *ciento*, from Latin *centum*); but there is no evidence for this before the fifth century A.D.; and even today the word for '100' is pronounced *kentu* in the Logudoro dialect of Sardinia.

This of course does not mean to say that Latin *c* represents an absolutely identical pronunciation in all environments. In

[1] It was, however, already familiar to the earliest of the Indian grammarians and phoneticians (Allen, *Phonetics in Ancient India*, 33 ff.). Quintilian (i, 4, 16) recommends the learning of the *t/d* distinction, but does not discuss it. In the middle ages the grammarian Hugutio still admits: 'licet enim *d* et *t* sint diuersae litterae, habent tamen adeo affinem sonum, quod ex sono non posset perpendi aliqua differentia'. Not until the nineteenth century is the distinction clearly understood in Europe.

English, for example, the initial sound in *kit* is articulated somewhat further forward on the palate than in *cat*, and is accompanied by a certain degree of lip-rounding* in *coot*. There is perhaps some actual evidence for this in Latin; an original short *e* followed by a 'dark' *l* (see p. 33) normally developed to a back* vowel, *o* or *u*—thus Old Latin *helus* becomes *holus*, and the past participle of *pello* is *pulsus*; but *scelus* does not change to *scolus*, and the past participle of the obsolete *cello* is *celsus*, not *culsus*; one possible explanation of this is that the change was prevented by the frontness of the preceding consonant.

In early Latin inscriptions *c* tends only to be used before *i* and *e*, *k* before consonants and *a* (retained in *Kalendae* and in the abbreviation *K.* for *Kaeso*), and *q* before *o* and *u*—e.g. *citra, feced; liktor, kaput; qomes, qura*—which is a further indication that the pronunciation varied somewhat according to environment; this practice is also found in some early Etruscan inscriptions. Such a complication, however, was clearly unnecessary; it is 'unphonemic' (see pp. 7 ff.) and would involve, if consistently employed, such variations as *loqus, loka, loci* within a single paradigm; and *c* was subsequently generalized in all environments, except in the consonantal combination *qu*.

The letter-shape ᴄ was ultimately derived from the Greek gamma (Γ), through a stage ⟨; but, as we have seen, it had come to be used in early Latin writing as a positional variant with ᴋ and ǫ (which it later supplanted) as a sign of the *voiceless* velar plosive /k/. This meant that there was no longer any distinctive sign for the voiced /g/ (hence inscriptional forms such as ᴠɪʀᴄᴏ for *uirgo*). In Etruscan, which perhaps provided the model for the Latin practice, this did not matter, since in that language voiced and voiceless plosives seem not to have been significantly distinguished. But in Latin the voiced /g/ contrasted with the voiceless /k/ (e.g. *lugere:lucere*); and the distinction between the two phonemes was eventually indicated by introducing the symbol ɢ for the voiced consonant (formed perhaps by the addition of a stroke to ᴄ).[1] The old spelling is,

---

[1] The device is traditionally attributed to Sp. Carvilius Ruga (third century B.C.), but it may go back to Appius Claudius in the late fourth century.

however, preserved in the abbreviations *C.* for *Gaius* and *Cn.* for *Gnaeus*.

qu The sound represented by this 'digraph' was of a type known technically as LABIO-VELAR, i.e. a velar plosive (such as that represented by Latin *c*) but with a simultaneous rounding and protrusion of the lips (as for English *w*); the phonetic symbol for such an articulation is [kʷ].

It is fairly certain that it was not a matter of two successive consonants as in e.g. English *quick*, where *qu* represents [kw]; for this we have some evidence in the grammarians, who speak of the *w*-element as being part of or blended (*confusa*) with the preceding letter (Pompeius, K. v, 104; Velius Longus, K. vii, 58; cf. Ter. Scaurus, K. vii, 16).[1] A statement of Marius Victorinus, though not altogether clear, seems in fact to distinguish the sound of *c* or *k* from that of *qu* simply by openness *versus* protrusion of the lips († K. vi, 34).

The grammarians' statements are supported by the fact that, with very rare exceptions, *qu* does not 'make position' in verse as it might be expected to, at least optionally, if it represented a sequence of two consonants; thus the first syllable of e.g. *equi* is always light. However, against this it could be argued that the treatment of certain groups as alternatively 'making position' is borrowed from Greek (see pp. 89f.), and that, unlike the groups plosive + liquid* (*tr*, etc.), a group [kw] had no parallel in Greek, which had lost its *w* at an early date.

Another fact which is sometimes cited as proof of the simultaneous nature of the *w*-element is that an *m* before *qu* may remain unchanged, whereas before *c* it is regularly changed to *n* (= [ŋ]; see p. 27); thus *horum + ce* gives *horunc*, *am + ceps* gives *anceps*, but *quam + quam* remains *quamquam* (similarly *quicumque*, *numquam*, *umquam*, etc.)—which suggests that the labial *w*-element was present from the start of the *qu*-sound, thereby providing an environment that favoured the preservation of the

---

[1] Quintilian's apparent citation of *quos* (i, 4, 10) as an example of consonantal *u* is probably a wrong reading (cf. Coleman, *CQ*, N.S. XIII (1963), 1).

preceding labial *m* (just as in e.g. *quamuis*),[1] in spite of the velar articulation of the stop* element. But the existence of alternative spellings with *n* (*quanquam*, etc.),[2] and the possibility that the *m* is due to analogical influence from *quam*, *cum*, etc. (as in e.g. *quamdiu* beside inscr. *quandiu*) diminishes the value of this evidence.

There are also historical arguments of two types. First, it is notable that, whereas in other environments the consonantal *u* [w] eventually became a fricative* [v], this change did not affect the *u* of *qu* (thus Italian *vero* but *quanto*); a difference is in fact already noticed by Velius Longus in the second century A.D. († K. vii, 58). Such a variation in development could of course be attributed simply to the fact that in *qu* the *u* occurs after a syllable-initial plosive, which is not the case in other occurrences of consonantal *u*[3] (except for *gu*; see below). But the very fact that no other such groups occur (i.e. no syllable-initial *p*, *b*, *t*, *d*+consonantal *u*) could itself be interpreted as an indication of the special nature of *qu* (and *gu*).[4] One may further cite here the statement of Priscian († K. ii, 7) that the *u* element of *qu*, when followed by a front vowel, has a special quality, like the Greek ʋ (i.e. like the initial sound of French *huit* as contrasted with *oui*)—whereas this is not stated to apply in the case of the independent consonant *u*.[5]

The other historical argument relates to the fact that in nearly all cases Latin *qu* derives from a single, labio-velar consonant of Indo-European, which is represented by single consonants of various kinds in other languages; thus Indo-

---

[1] Also in e.g. inscr. *comualem* (117 B.C.), which preserves the old prefix *com-* (later *con-*).

[2] Favoured by Pliny the Elder, according to Priscian (K. ii, 29).

[3] In compounds such as *aduenio*, *subuenio*, the syllabic division falls between the *d* or *b* and the consonantal *u*, giving regularly heavy quantity to the preceding syllable (cf. p. 89).

[4] It was already so interpreted by the grammarians Pompeius and Ps.-Sergius in their commentaries on Donatus (K. iv, 367; iv, 476; v, 104), though their arguments are misunderstood by Bede (K. vii, 228).

[5] This is confirmed also for the classical period by Greek inscriptional spellings such as Κυιντιλιος, Ακυλ(λ)ιος for *Quintilius*, *Aquilius* (Augustus or earlier), with κυι or κυ for *qui*, as against κουα or κοα regularly for *qua*. No such spelling is found for simple *ui* [wi]; cf. Eckinger, *Die Orthographie lateinischer Wörter in griechischen Inschriften*. See also p. 52 below.

European *kʷod* gives, beside Latin *quod*, Sanskrit *kad*: Oscan *púd*: English *what* (where *wh* is pronounced either [hʷ] or simply [w]). However, this argument is slightly weakened by the fact that in *equus* the *qu* derives from an Indo-European group *kw*, which is represented by a group or double consonant in some other languages (e.g. Sanskrit *aśvas*: Greek ἵππος).

The various arguments, at least on balance, clearly favour the pronunciation of *qu* as a single, labio-velar consonant [kʷ]. Consonants of this type are common in a number of languages, e.g. at the present day in Caucasian, African, and American Indian languages, and in ancient times in Mycenaean Greek; and they present no particular difficulty of pronunciation. On the other hand no confusion is caused if the Latin *qu* is pronounced in the same way as English, since a sequence of [k] and [w] does not otherwise occur in Latin (though it does in some of the languages mentioned above, including Mycenaean). It is possible in any case that an alternative pronunciation of this kind may actually have existed in some varieties of Latin speech. In Lucretius, for example, some occurrences of the forms *ăquae* and *ăquai* are probably to be read with heavy first syllable; this is certainly true of *lĭquidus* in some cases;[1] and such treatment becomes more common in Latin poetry after the fourth century A.D. This might indicate a pronunciation of *qu* as a consonant-group [kw]—as is assumed for the Lucretian examples by the grammarian Audax (K. vii, 328 f.); on the other hand, it may simply reflect the beginning of a dialectal tendency to lengthen the stop element to [kk]—a tendency reproved in the fourth century by the *Appendix Probi* (K. iv, 198; 'aqua, non acqua'), though with little effect to judge by Italian *acqua*.

There remains one further peculiarity connected with *qu*, the discussion of which requires a certain amount of preliminary explanation. Under various conditions, and probably at various times, Old Latin short *o* became classical *u* (e.g. during the third century B.C. in final syllables, so that *primŏs* became *primus*, etc.). Where, however, the *ŏ* was preceded by *u* (vowel or consonant), or by *qu* or *ngu*, these changes do not appear in

---

[1] (for *aqua*) vi, 552, 868, 1072; (for *liquidus*) i, 349; iii, 427; iv, 1259.

writing until the end of the republic. Until then inscriptions still show such forms as *uolgus, auonculus, seruos, perspicuos, equos*, instead of *uulgus*, etc. Scholars are divided in opinion as to whether the spelling with *uo* really represents the pronunciation, or whether it was preserved merely to avoid the ambiguous writing of two successive *u* symbols,[1] which might possibly be interpreted as a single long vowel[2] (cf. p. 64). The latter explanation may not appear altogether convincing, but the practice does seem to have an orthographic rather than a genuine phonetic basis; for when the change of *o* to *u* does eventually take place in the spelling of such words, it affects all cases equally, whatever the phonetic conditions; thus words of the type *seruŏs* (final syllable), *uolgus* (before *l* + consonant), *auonculus* (before [ŋ]), all equally start to appear as *seruus*, *uulgus, auunculus*, etc., in inscriptions of the Augustan period.

The old spelling is found not only in inscriptions, but also in some manuscript traditions, as of Plautus and Terence, and even Vergil and Horace. But wherever *uo* is found for later *uu* in classical Latin, it is certainly to be pronounced as *uu* in imperial times, and almost certainly earlier. This does not of course apply to those cases where *uŏ* is invariable; thus, although *uolt* is to be read as *uult, uolo* is to be pronounced as written.

In the case of Old Latin *quo* and *nguo*, however (as in e.g. *equos, unguont*), a further development is involved; for when the change to *quu, nguu* took place, the new *u* vowel had the effect of causing a dissimilatory loss of the preceding *u* element: thus *quu, nguu* became *cu, ngu*.[3] This phonetic change

---

[1] The writing with *o*, however, does of course involve a secondary ambiguity, since if vowel-length is not marked, *seruos* could stand for nominative singular or accusative plural.

[2] Thus Quintilian i, 4, 10; cf. i, 7, 26 and Velius Longus, K. vii, 58 f. Conversely, towards the end of the republic, *uu* came to be written where a single *u* would give rise to ambiguity: thus, for example, *iuuenis, fluuius*, as against earlier inscr. *iuenta, fluio*, etc., where the *i* might be read wrongly as a vowel in the first word and a consonant in the second (no such ambiguity arises, however, in a form such as *fluit*, which therefore continues to be so written).

[3] A similar loss of consonantal *u* before *u* vowels probably occurred in other cases also: thus, beginning at the end of the republic, occasional inscriptional forms such as *aeum, uius, serus* for *aeuum, uiuus, seruus*. But in such cases analogical pressure (from *serui*, etc.) rapidly restored the lost *u* both in writing and in educated

CONSONANTS

is largely obscured by analogical spelling (e.g. *equos* or *equus* continuing to be written for *ecus* after the analogy of such forms as the plural *equi*); but the true situation is revealed by occasional inscriptional forms with *c*, and later confirmed by the grammarians, who, though they support the analogical spellings, are nevertheless clear that they do not correspond to the pronunciation. Thus (first century A.D.) Cornutus (Cassiodor(i)us, K. vii, 150 f.): 'extinguunt per duo *u*...extinguo est enim, et ab hoc extinguunt, licet enuntiari non possit'; (second century A.D.) Velius Longus (K. vii, 59): 'auribus quidem sufficiebat ut equus per unum *u* scriberetur, ratio tamen duo exigit'.

This dissimilatory loss of *u* may well have been an immediate consequence of the change of *ŏ* to *u*; so that in classical Latin wherever one finds *quu* or *nguu* (or *quo*, *nguo* in the older spelling), they probably represent a pronunciation *cu*, *ngu*. Thus *equus* or *equos* probably stands for *ecus*, *quum* or *quom* for *cum*, *sequuntur* or *sequontur* for *secuntur*, *unguunt* or *unguont* for *ungunt*, etc. But no doubt there were analogical pronunciations, as well as spellings, of the type *equus*, and such a pronunciation is also therefore probably admissible.[1]

No problem of course arises in the case of words like *quod*, *sequor*, where there is never any change of *ŏ* to *u*, and which are therefore always to be pronounced as written.[2]

(ii) Voiced* plosives

There are four varieties of these in Latin, parallel to the voiceless series, and represented by *b*, *d*, *g*, and *gu* respectively. The

speech (except in *boum*, genitive plural of *bos*, which became normal). The forms without consonantal *u* evidently survived, however, in some forms of popular speech (cf. *Appendix Probi*, '*riuus* non *rius*', and Italian *rio*).

[1] There remains the possibility that before an *u*-vowel *c* and *g* were in any case pronounced as [kʷ], [gʷ], with an automatic *w*-element. In which case it is not so much a matter of dissimilation as of 'neutralization', i.e. absence of difference between *cu/ngu* and *quu/nguu*.

[2] The pronunciation of *quoque* ('also') is sometimes questioned. Quintilian reports, as a pun in bad taste, Cicero's words to a candidate whose father was a cook: 'Ego quoque tibi fauebo' (vi, 3, 47), which seems to suggest that *quoque* was pronounced *coque* (similarly in *Anthol.* 199, 96). Etymologically this is a possible form (cf. *cottidie*), but it is not otherwise attested, and other interpretations are possible.

20

grammarians, as we have seen in the case of the t/d pair (p. 13), failed to discover the nature of 'voice'; thus d is said to differ from t in that it represents a pure dental. It may well in fact be true that d was pronounced as a dental, but we can no more safely rely on the grammarians' statements of this than we can on their descriptions of t as an alveolar. The difference between b and p, and between g and c, is expressed in terms that could be interpreted as referring to a difference in muscular tension, which commonly supplements the voice difference (e.g. † Marius Victorinus, K. vi, 33). But in some cases the writer is clearly at a loss to explain the nature of the distinction—thus Martianus Capella (3, 261): '*B* labris per spiritus impetum reclusis edicamus....*P* labris spiritus erumpit'.

b, *d* and *g*, then, have close affinities to the voiced sounds represented by English *b*, *d* and 'hard' *g*.

In some cases, however, *b* is written instead of *p* for the *voiceless* plosive—namely before the voiceless sounds of *t* and *s* under certain special conditions. It is so used when the voiceless sound occurs at the end of a preposition or noun-stem which, in other environments, ends in a voiced *b*. Thus in e.g. *obtineo, obsideo, subsideo, absoluo, trabs, urbs, plebs, caelebs*, the *b* is in fact partially assimilated to the following *t* or *s*, becoming voiceless [p]; but it continues to be written with a *b* by analogy with forms such as *obeo, urbis*, etc. (similarly the preposition *abs* owes its writing with *b* rather than *p* to the alternative form *ab*); in inscriptions one even occasionally finds such forms as *scribtura* (with *b* after *scribo*).

On general phonetic grounds it is highly probable that the *b* before *t* or *s* should stand for [p]. It is moreover expressly stated by Quintilian (i, 7, 7) and other grammarians, and clearly indicated by inscriptional spellings with *p* at all periods (e.g. *pleps, opsides, apsoluere, suptilissima, optinebit*). The distinction between spelling and speech is clearly summed up by Quintilian in the words: '*b* litteram ratio poscit, aures magis audiunt *p*'; and on the writing of *abs* Velius Longus comments (K. vii, 62): 'qui originem uerborum propriam respiciunt, per *b* scribunt'.

Similar considerations apply to the spellings *bf* (*obfero*, etc.), *bm* (*submoueo*, etc.), *bg* (*obgero*, etc.), *bc* (*subcingo*, etc.), and *br* in the case of the preposition *sub* (*subripio*, etc.), though here the assimilation is complete, giving a pronunciation *offero*, *summoueo*, *oggero*, *succingo*, *surripio*, etc.

Similarly also analogical spelling with *d* is found in the case of the preposition *ad*. It is fairly certain that in most cases the *d* was completely assimilated to the following consonant in speech (except *h*, *i*, *u*, or *m*); so that spellings of the type *adsequor*, *adtineo*, *adripio*, *adfui*, *adpono*, *adgredior*, *adcurro* were probably pronounced as *assequor*, *attineo*, *arripio*, *affui*, *appono*, *aggredior*, *accurro*, etc. Apart from the existence of these latter spellings alongside the analogical *adsequor*, etc., one may cite the pun in Plautus (*Po.* 279):

M. Assum apud te eccum.

A. At ego elixus sis uolo,

which involves a play on *assum* (*ad-sum*) 'I am present' and *assum* 'roasted'. The question of such spellings is raised by Lucilius (375 Marx), though he dismisses it as unimportant:

...accurrere scribas

d-ne an *c* non est quod quaeras....

As Velius Longus (*loc. cit.*) comments, 'ille quidem non putauit interesse scripturae; sed si sonus consulitur, interest aurium ut *c* potius quam *d* scribatur'.

In the case of *dl*, however (e.g. *adloqui*), the same grammarian does permit a pronunciation as such, as well as the assimilated *alloqui*. It is in fact uncertain to what extent in educated speech the analogical spellings may also have been reflected in pronunciation. What is virtually certain is that, even when this happened, the *b* or *d* will have been devoiced to [p] or [t] before a following voiceless sound—so that the analogical pronunciation would actually be of the type *opfero*, *supcingo*, *atsequor*, *atfui*, *atpono*, *atcurro*, rather than *obfero*, etc.

g As in the case of *c*, this never implies a 'soft' pronunciation. The evidence is parallel to that for *c* (e.g. Greek Γελλιος =

Gellius; *ingerunt* cited as an example of the velar nasal); there is no evidence for any change before *e* and *i* until around 500 A.D. As with *c*, however, some slight variation is probable according to the following vowel (as in English *gear, guard, gourd*); the fact that *gelu* does not become *golu* may indicate a fronted pronunciation before *e* (see p. 15).

In one particular environment, however, *g* seems to have had a markedly different value. In the position before the dental nasal* *n* (e.g. *agnus, dignus, regnum*) it is probable that it represented a velar *nasal* sound [ŋ], like that of *ng* in English *hang* or *n* in *bank*: so that *gn* in a word like *agnus* would be pronounced like the *ngn* of an English word like *hangnail*.

This would be in line with a general tendency of Latin to nasalize plosives before *n* (note e.g. Latin *somnus* = Sanskrit *svapnas*, with Latin change of *p* to *m* before *n*).[1] It is also indicated by inscriptional spellings such as *ingnes, ingnominiae* for *ignes, ignominiae*. It would further explain why an *n* appears to be lost in such forms as *ignosco* (= *in* + *gnosco*) or *cognatus* (= *con* + *gnatus*); for

   (*a*) before velar sounds we know from the grammarians that *n* represented a velar [ŋ] (see p. 27);

   (*b*) if *gn* in fact represents [ŋn], then a combination *con* + *gnatus* would theoretically imply a pronunciation [koŋŋnātus];

but before another consonant the double [ŋŋ] would then be simplified to [ŋ], giving [koŋnātus] (N.B. inscr. *congnatus*); and such a pronunciation would be represented by a spelling *cognatus*.

Further evidence comes from words of the type *dignus, lignum, ilignus*. The words from which these are derived—*decet, lego, ilex*—all have a short *e* vowel, and it is necessary to explain the change of *ĕ* to *ĭ*. Now such a change does regularly take place before the sound [ŋ]; beside Greek τέγγω [teŋgō], for example, the cognate Latin verb is *tinguo*; and whereas *con* + *scando* gives *conscendo, con* + *tango* gives *contingo* (there is a parallel to this in the Middle English change of [e] to [i] in such words as *England*). The change of vowel in *dignus*, etc., there-

[1] Cf. also inscr. *amnegauerit* for *abnegauerit*.

23

fore, is explained if *g* had here the value [ŋ]. The absence of any such change in words like *regnum, segnis* is due to the fact that the vowel is here *long* (cf. Latin *rēx* and Greek ἧκα respectively), and so is not affected by the change.

Of little primary value, but of interest as confirmatory evidence, is the play on words in Plautus (*Ru.* 767) between *ignem magnum* and *inhumanum*, and in Cicero (*Rep.* iv, 6) between *ignominia* and *in nomine*—both of which at least suggest a nasal value for *g*.

However, the awkward fact still remains that the developments in most Romance languages are better explained by assuming the normal [g] rather than the nasal value for *g* in the group *gn*. Thus *lignum* develops in exactly the same way as *nigrum* in e.g. Old French *lein/neir*, Engadine *lain/nair*, S. Italian *liunu/niuru* (the *g* in each case having undergone a change to *i* or *u* before the following consonant). An important exception, nevertheless, is the conservative Sardinian, with e.g. *linna, mannu, konnadu* from Latin *ligna, magnum, cognatum* (cf. Latin inscr. *sinnu* for *signum*).

The grammarians also are strangely silent about any nasal pronunciation of *g*, and in initial position Terentianus Maurus seems to suggest the normal [g] value in the name *Gnaeus* when, referring to the spelling of the name with *Cn.*, he says

g tamen sonabit illic quando *Gnaeum* enuntio

(K. vi, 351).

But in fact by this time any pronunciation of the initial *G* must have been artificial; as Varro already observes (fr. 330 Funaioli), 'qui *G* littera in hoc praenomine utuntur, antiquitatem sequi uidentur'. Varro also notes a spelling *Naeum* (and Ναιος is common in Greek).

A solution to the apparent contradiction of evidence for the pronunciation of *gn* was proposed by C. D. Buck, who suggested that the nasal pronunciation of *g* as [ŋ] was in fact the normal development, but that subsequently a 'spelling pronunciation' was introduced, first in educated circles, then more generally, whereby *g* was given its more common [g] value. At what period such a change took place it is impossible to say, but Sardinian suggests that it was very late, and for the classical period the nasal pronunciation remains the more probable. What must be emphasized, however, is that at no period of Latin was *gn* pronounced as a 'palatal' [ñ], as in modern Italian or French and as in the national pronunciation of Latin by speakers of these languages.

A note on the pronunciation of Latin *gn* in England will be found at the end of Appendix B.

It is generally assumed that *g* did not have a nasal pronunciation before *m*, as in *tegmen, segmentum*, since the change of *ě* to *ĭ* does not occur in these words. However, since original *gm* seems to have given *mm* (e.g. *flamma* from *flag-ma*, cf. *flagro*), all examples of *gm* may have arisen later, e.g. by syncope, after the change of *ě* to *ĭ* was operative (cf. the unsyncopated forms *tegimen, integumentum*). The possibility of a pronunciation of *g* as [ŋ] here is therefore not entirely excluded—though it cannot be safely recommended.

gu On the grounds of its graphic parallelism with *qu*, we might expect that Latin *gu* (with consonantal *u*) also represents a single, labio-velar consonant [gʷ], rather than a sequence [gw]. It is, however, less easy to demonstrate this, since the grammarians do not specifically discuss the matter, and the combination occurs only after *n* (as in *lingua*), where the preceding syllable is in any case heavy and so can give no clue. However, in view of the fact that all other plosive consonants in Latin occur in pairs, voiceless and voiced (*p/b*, etc.), it is to be expected that the voiceless [kʷ] would have a voiced counterpart [gʷ]; and there seems in fact to be an indirect indication of this parallelism in a passage of Priscian already referred to (p. 17 above). For after mentioning a special quality of the *u* element of *qu* when followed by a front vowel, he goes on specifically to say that the same applies to the *u* element of *gu*.

(iii) Aspirates*

The digraphs *ph, th, ch* represented aspirated voiceless plosives—not unlike the initial sounds of *pot, top, cot* respectively (see p. 12). They occupy a peculiar place in the orthographic system, since they are not found in the earliest inscriptions and make their appearance only about the middle of the second century B.C. They are then used, and become standard, primarily in transcribing Greek names and loan-words containing aspirated plosives (φ, θ, χ), e.g. *Philippus, philtrum, Corinthus, cithara, thesaurus, Achaea, bacchanal, machina, chorus*; and in such cases it is likely that educated Roman speakers in fact reproduced the Greek aspirates with more or less fidelity. Before this time the Greek aspirates had been transcribed in Latin by simple *p, t, c* (e.g. inscr. *Pilemo, Corinto, Antioco*), and this spelling remains normal in some early borrowings from Greek (e.g. *purpura* = πορφύρα, *tus* = θύος, *calx* = χάλιξ). But subsequently (beginning in fact, on inscriptional evidence, already by the end of the second century B.C.) aspirates made their appearance in a number of native Latin words (and loan-words without an original aspirate): thus in *pulcher, lachrima, sepulchrum, bracchium, triumphus, Gracchus* (also in the place-name *Carthago*), less generally in *lurcho, anchora, Orchus*, and occasionally in inscriptional forms such as *chorona, centhurio, praecho, archa, trichlinium, exerchitator, fulchra, Olymphi, Volchanus, Marchus, Calphurnius*—note also the Greek spelling Σολφικιος (from early first century A.D.), as well as Πο(υ)λχερ (first in mid first century B.C. and frequent later).

We know from a statement of Cicero († *Or.* 160) that in his time an actual change in the pronunciation of many such words was taking place, and he himself came to accept *pulcher, triumphus, Carthago*, though rejecting *sepulchrum, chorona, lachrima, Orchiuius*. The grammarians show a good deal of disagreement (e.g. † Mar. Vict., K. vi, 21; Ter. Scaurus, K. vii, 20), and it would be easy to dismiss the aspirated pronunciation as a mere fashionable misapplication of Greek speech-habits. That such tendencies did in fact exist we know from Catullus' poem about

Arrius, with his pronunciation of *commoda* as *chommoda*, etc. But it is remarkable that in nearly all the attested cases the aspiration occurs in the vicinity of a 'liquid' consonant (*r* or *l*).[1] It seems more probable, therefore, that the aspiration represents a special but natural environmental development in Latin itself,[2] which may possibly have varied in different areas and social strata. Had the digraphs not been introduced to represent the Greek aspirates in the first place, Latin would have had no need to indicate the aspiration of *pulc(h)er*, etc., in writing, since it was merely an automatic variant of the normal voiceless stops (just as we do not need to indicate the aspiration of initial voiceless stops in English). But once the digraphs had been introduced in order more accurately to represent the pronunciation of loan-words from Greek, it would be natural enough to employ them also for writing similar sounds in Latin.

The practical outcome of these discussions is as follows. An English pronunciation of Latin *p*, *t*, *c*, though not intolerable, will certainly be rather more aspirated than the Latin. And some special effort is therefore required in pronouncing the aspirates *ph*, *th*, *ch*, if these are to sound distinct from *p*, *t*, *c*. It should perhaps also be emphasized that there is no justification for pronouncing the aspirates as fricatives*—i.e. as in *photo*, *thick*, *loch*; this is admittedly the value of φ, θ, χ in Late Greek, but it had not yet developed by classical Latin times.

(iv) Nasals*

n Most commonly this stands for a dental (or alveolar) nasal sound [n], similar to the *n* in English *net* or *tent*, e.g. in *nego*, *bonus*, *ante*, *inde*.

Before a velar or a labio-velar, however (as in *uncus*, *ingens*, *relinquo*, *lingua*), it stands for a velar nasal [ŋ] (as in English *uncle* or *anger*). Quite apart from the general expectation that it would be assimilated in this way, there is clear evidence in

---

[1] For a more technical discussion of similar effects elsewhere in the history of Latin and some other languages cf. *Archivum Linguisticum*, x (1958), 110 ff.

[2] Aspiration in some proper names, e.g. *Cethegus*, *Otho*, *Matho*, may perhaps be of Etruscan origin (Cicero accepts aspiration only for the first of these).

ancient descriptions, the earliest of which goes back to Accius (second century B.C.), who wished to follow Greek practice by writing e.g. *aggulus, agcora* for *angulus, ancora* (†Varro, cited by Priscian, K. ii, 30).[1] In the first century B.C. Nigidius Figulus not ineptly described the sound as 'intermediate between *n* and *g*' (†Gellius, xix, 14, 7).

The same [ŋ] sound almost certainly occurred when the preposition *in* was followed by a word beginning with a velar or labio-velar (e.g. *in causa*). Similarly, when followed by a labial (*p, b, m*) it was pronounced *m*, as shown by inscriptional *im pace, im balneum, im muro*.

In words like *consul*, where the *n* is followed by the fricative *s*, one would certainly not be wrong in pronouncing it normally; but other pronunciations were current even among educated persons in classical times. At a very early period *n* in such an environment had lost its consonantal value (a common development in many languages) and had been replaced by a mere nasalization of the preceding vowel, which was at the same time lengthened by way of compensation for the lost consonant. Thus *consol, censor* became *cõsol, cẽsor*. As a result, in the earliest inscriptions one often finds spellings of the type *cosol* (whence the archaistic abbreviation *cos.*), *cesor, cosentiont*, etc.,[2] alongside the spellings with *n*. In popular speech the nasalization was eventually lost, and we are told that even Cicero used to pronounce some such words without an *n*, e.g. *forēsia, Megalēsia, hortēsia* (Velius Longus, K. vii, 79). In Vulgar Latin it must have been completely lost, for there is no sign of

---

[1] By one widely held view of phonemic theory, the [ŋ] would have to be considered as belonging to a separate phoneme from [n], since the two sounds occur in contrast in *annus/agnus* (see p. 23). But one can also take the view that in e.g. *ancora* the [ŋ] is an allophone of /n/ and in *agnus* an allophone of /g/. Such an interpretation is reflected in the Latin orthography; the Greek practice, however (e.g. in ἄγγος, ἄγκυρα), identifies the [ŋ] before a velar with the [ŋ] which occurs before a nasal in e.g. πρᾶγμα and is there interpreted as an allophone of the /g/ phoneme—hence the spelling with γ in both cases. The Greek practice is ambiguous only in the case of ἔγγονος, where the first γ in fact has the value [g], and which no doubt for this reason is generally written ἔκγονος. In Latin such a practice, as advocated by Accius, would be made ambiguous by the existence of such words as *agger*.

[2] Note also Greek transcriptions such as Ὁρτήσιος, Κλήμης, Κησορινος for *Hortensius, Clemens, Censorinus*.

it whatever in the derived words in the Romance languages (e.g. Italian *mese, sposa* from *mē(n)sis, spō(n)sa*).

But in the official orthography the *n* was preserved or restored, and this had its effect on most educated speech of the classical period. Probably few speakers, however, were entirely consistent, and their inconsistencies provided a happy hunting ground for later grammarians; in Caper, for example (K. vii, 95), we find the quite artificial rule: 'omnia adverbia numeri sine *n* scribenda sunt, ut *milies, centies, decies; quotiens, totiens* per *n* scribenda sunt'. One is reminded of the 'rules' about the use of *shall* and *will* in English (while these were being crystallized by the grammarians between the seventeenth and early nineteenth century, the actual usage was erratic—in fact even in written English *will* was about twice as common as *shall* in the first person!). The only safe practical rule for the modern reader in regard to Latin *ns* is to pronounce the *n* wherever it is written.

The same considerations apply to cases where *n* is followed by the other Latin fricative, *f*; hence inscriptional forms such as *cofeci, iferos* for *confeci, inferos*. In the classical forms with restored *n*, however, the *n* here probably stands not for a dental or alveolar nasal but rather for a *labio-dental**, formed by contact of the lower lip and upper teeth in the same way as the following *f*. Pronunciations of this kind are common for some English speakers in words like *comfort, information*. In Latin the variation in republican inscriptions between *n* and *m* in such cases (e.g. *infimo, infectei, confice,* beside *eimferis, comfluont,* and even *im fronte*) clearly points to such a pronunciation; and although the spelling with *n* was later generalized, the labio-dental pronunciation probably continued.

Wherever the nasal consonant was pronounced before *s* or *f*, it is certainly to be considered as a more or less artificial restoration, rather than a natural retention. For, as already mentioned, when the *n* was lost it gave rise to a lengthening of the preceding vowel; but the classical pronunciation WITH *n* also has a long vowel (for evidence see p. 65), which shows that the *n* must first have been lost, and subsequently restored. The development in a word such as *consul*, therefore, is:

prehistoric *cŏnsol*; early Latin *cõsol*; classical colloquial *cōsul*; classical literary *cōnsul*.

As might be expected, the difference between popular speech and official spelling in this matter gave rise to occasional spellings in which *n* was introduced where it had never in fact been spoken, e.g. *thensaurus* (=Greek θησαυρός), *occansio*, *Herculens*, all of which are specifically proscribed by the grammarians. Such spellings may of course in turn have led to occasional pronunciations based upon them.

m At the beginning and in the interior of words the sound represented by *m* presents no problem. It stands for a bilabial nasal, as in e.g. English *mat* or *camp*. There are, however, points to notice where it occurs at the ends of words. In general it seems to have been reduced (like the *n* before a fricative internally) to a mere nasalization of the preceding vowel—in the imprecise terminology of the grammarians it is 'almost a foreign letter' (†Velius Longus, K. vii, 54), or 'obscurum in extremitate dictionum sonat' (Priscian, K. ii, 29); and in early inscriptions one often finds the final *m* omitted, e.g. in the third-century epitaph of L. Corn. Scipio:

> honc oino ploirume cosentiont...
> ˙duonoro optumo fuise uiro

(=hunc unum plurimi consentiunt...bonorum optimum fuisse uirum). In the course of the second century, the official spelling established the writing of final *m*; but forms without *m* continued occasionally to be found.

That the vowel was lengthened as well as nasalized is suggested by the fact that such final syllables, when followed by an initial consonant, count as heavy—thus, for example, *Ῑtaliam fātō = Ῑtaliã fātō*. An indication of this lengthening is also perhaps seen in Cato the Elder's writing of *diem* as *diee* (Quintilian, ix, 4, 39).[1]

The non-consonantal nature of final *m* is also shown by the

---

[1] It has, however, been suggested that Cato's second E may have been an M written sideways.

fact that syllables so ending are elided in verse in the same way as if they ended in a vowel (with rare exceptions: e.g. Ennius *milia militum octo*: cf. p. 81, n. 3); from which one concludes that they simply ended in a nasalized vowel. For the *m* in this position, when followed by an initial vowel, Verrius Flaccus is said to have favoured writing a half-*m* (Λ) only (Velius Longus, K. vii, 80); Quintilian (†ix, 4, 40) describes it as hardly pronounced; and later grammarians refer to it as being completely lost (e.g. †Velius Longus, K. vii, 54). If elision involves complete loss of the final vowel (cf. p. 78) the distinction between nasalized and non-nasalized in this context is of course purely academic.

The same treatment of final *m* is seen in cases of 'aphaeresis', where inscriptions regularly omit it (e.g. *scriptust* for *scriptum est*).

It is of interest that preferences regarding the elision of vowel + *m* are the same as for long vowels or diphthongs[1]— a further indication that the vowel was in fact not only nasalized but lengthened.[2]

Where, however, a final *m* was followed by a closely connected word beginning with a stop (plosive or nasal) consonant, it seems to have been treated rather as in the interior of a word, being assimilated to the following consonant (in this case, naturally, without lengthening of the preceding vowel). Thus we find inscriptional *tan durum* for *tam durum* (and in e.g. *tam grauis* we may assume a parallel assimilation to the following velar, giving [ŋ] for *m*); Velius Longus says that in *etiam nunc* 'plenius per *n* quam per *m* enuntiatur'; and Cicero also refers to unfortunate *doubles entendres* in such phrases as *cum nobis* (*Or.*, 154; *Fam.*, ix, 22, 2).

---

[1] Thus in Vergil, *Aen.* i, elisions of final short vowels total (*a*) before a heavy syllable 132, (*b*) before a light syllable 39; corresponding figures for final long vowels and diphthongs are (*a*) 81, (*b*) 5; and for syllables with final *m*, (*a*) 90, (*b*) 7. For all hexameters from Ennius to Ovid elisions before light syllables total 3947 for short vowels, 416 for long vowels and diphthongs, and 514 for syllables with final *m*.

[2] Before final *m* a vowel is never inherently long, since any such long vowels had been shortened in early Latin (cf. p. 74).

31

(v) Liquids

This title is commonly given to the *r* and *l* sounds of Latin (and indeed generally). It is ultimately derived, through the Latin translation *liquidus*, from the Greek ὑγρός 'fluid'; this rather peculiar term was applied by the Greek grammarians to the consonants *r*, *l*, *n*, and *m*, in reference to the fact that when they follow a plosive (as, for example, *tr*), they permit the quantity of a preceding syllable containing a short vowel to be 'doubtful' —as in Greek πατρός, Latin *patris*, etc. In Latin, however, this does not apply to *n* and *m*, and so the term 'liquid' has come to have a more restricted sense.

r The pronunciation of *r* is liable to cause some difficulty to speakers of standard southern English, since in this form of speech the *r*-sound occurs only before vowels; otherwise it has been lost, with compensatory lengthening of the preceding vowel in stressed syllables—thus, for example, *harbour bar* is pronounced [hābə bā]. If such habits are carried over into Latin they result in a loss of distinction between e.g. *parcis* and *pācis* (both being pronounced [pākis]). Wherever an *r* is written in Latin, it is to be pronounced, without lengthening of the preceding vowel—a practice that will present less difficulty to Scottish and many other dialect speakers.

The precise quality of the Latin *r*-sound, however, has still to be considered—the English dialects include such wide variations as retroflex or retracted (in the west country, Ireland, and America), uvular (in Northumberland and Durham), tapped and fricative (in the south). There is evidence that the Latin *r* was of the tongue-tip 'trilled' or 'rolled' type common in Scotland and some parts of northern England. Apart from imprecise early descriptions of the sound as being like the growling of a dog (e.g. † Lucilius, 377 f. Marx), we have clear reference to its vibrant nature in the later grammarians: in the words of Terentianus Maurus (K. vi, 332), 'uibrat tremulis ictibus aridum sonorem' (similarly †Mar. Vict., K. vi, 34).

It is true that at earlier periods the pronunciation may have been different. The change of Latin *s* between vowels *via* [z] to *r* (e.g. *dirimo* from *dis-emo, gero* beside *gestus*) suggests a fricative value for *r* (as in the southern English pronunciation of *draw*); and the change of *d* to *r* in Old Latin inscr. *aruorsum* for *aduorsum*, etc., suggests a 'tapped' articulation[1] (i.e. a single stroke as against the repeated strokes of a trill). But the former change is datable to the mid fourth century at latest (see p. 35), and the latter to the second century at latest. By the classical period there is no reason to think that the sound had not strengthened to the trill described by later writers.

r is normally assimilated to a following *l* (e.g. *intellego* from *inter-lego*); the *r* is sometimes restored, as in *perlego*—but according to Velius Longus (K. vii, 65), so far as *per* is concerned, it was a mark 'elegantioris sermonis' to pronounce as *pellego*, etc.

During the first century B.C. the spelling *rh-, -rrh-* was introduced to render the Greek ῥ-, -ῤῥ-, standing for *voiceless* [r], single and double respectively,—e.g. *Rhegium, Pyrrhus*. Whether Latin speakers ever so pronounced them seems doubtful, and spellings are found with false *rh* (becoming regular in *Rhenus*, which in fact derives from a Celtic *rēnos*).

1 This also represents a tongue-tip (dental or alveolar) sound, but with the lateral* articulation typical of *l*-sounds in English and other languages. In fact in the classical period its pronunciation seems to have been especially like that of the English *l*.

In English this sound has two main varieties—a so-called 'clear' *l*, which occurs before vowels (as e.g. in *look, silly*), and a 'dark' *l* which occurs elsewhere (thus before a consonant in *field*, and finally in *hill*). The 'dark' *l* involves a raising of the back part of the tongue (in addition to the front contact), whereas the 'clear' *l* involves no such raising. This difference in articulation gives rise to different acoustic impressions, the 'dark' *l* having an inherent resonance like that of a back vowel (*u, o*), and the 'clear' *l* like that of a front vowel (*i, e*).

Much the same situation evidently prevailed in Latin. The grammarians' statements are not very precise, but Pliny the

[1] Similarly in the normal *meridies* for *medi-dies*.

Elder's observations on this matter († Priscian, K. ii, 29) include mention of a special pronunciation at the ends of words (as in *sol*) and of syllables, i.e. before another consonant (as in *silua*). Pliny describes this special quality by the term '*plenus*', to which corresponds the term '*pinguis*' in a later grammarian (Consentius); by both writers this is contrasted with an '*exilis*' quality in other environments.[1] Now elsewhere the terms '*plenus*' and '*pinguis*' are used to refer to the acoustic quality of back vowels, as against '*exilis*' for front vowels (cf. Velius Longus, K. vii, 49 f.); it thus becomes clear that this special quality of *l* was the same 'dark' quality as for the English *l* in similar environments.

This also fits in with certain prehistoric changes of vowel-quality associated with *l*. For before pre-consonantal and final *l* we find a change of front vowels to back—thus *uelim* (with 'clear' *l*) remains unchanged, but original *ueltis* becomes *uoltis* (later *uultis*) under the influence of the back-vowel resonance of the 'dark' *l*.[2] At this time, to judge from such developments as *uolo* from original *uelo*, or *famulus* beside *familia*, a 'dark' *l* was prevalent also before vowels other than front vowels. But this latter tendency seems to have ended by the classical period.

We are thus able to reconstruct the different pronunciations of Latin *l* with some accuracy—only to conclude that the rules are basically the same as for modern English. It is therefore entirely appropriate in this case to follow English speech-habits, pronouncing the *l* in *facul* as in *pull*, in *facultas* as in *consultant*, and in *facilis* as in *penniless*.

(vi) Fricatives*

f The English *f* represents a labio-dental* sound, formed by the upper teeth and lower lip, and there is clear evidence that the same applied to classical Latin; such a pronunciation is suggested by Quintilian († xii, 10, 29), and more clearly indicated by the later grammarians (e.g. Mar. Vict., K. vi, 34:

---

[1] According to Pliny this applied particularly to the second of two *l*'s (as in *ille*).

[2] In late Latin the 'dark' *l* was actually replaced by *u* in some areas, e.g. inscr. *Aubia = Albia*; this development is reflected in some of the Romance languages, e.g. French *autre* from *alterum*. Cf. also Cockney [miwk] for *milk*, etc.

'*F* litteram imum labrum superis imprimentes dentibus...leni spiramine proferemus').

It is sometimes suggested that in early Latin, and even into late republican times, it was pronounced as a *bilabial*, i.e. by the two lips, without intervention of the teeth; and occasional inscriptional spellings such as *im fronte, comfluont* are cited as supporting this by having *m*, which is a bilabial, instead of *n*. But even if such examples were more common, the evidence would be quite inconclusive; for the preceding nasal can well have had a *labio-dental* articulation (cf. p. 29), and it is then purely a matter of orthographical convention whether it is represented by the sign of the normally bilabial *m* or the normally dental *n*.

s This represents in Latin a voiceless alveolar fricative ('sibilant') not unlike the English *s* in *sing* or *ss* in *lesson*. This is clear from grammarians' statements referring to a hissing sound formed by a constriction behind the teeth (e.g. Ter. Maurus, K. vi, 332; Mar. Vict., K. vi, 34). But it is most important to note that, unlike the English *s*, it stands for a *voiceless* consonant in all positions; it is not voiced between vowels or at word-end as in English *roses* (phonetically [rouziz]). Thus Latin *causae* is to be pronounced as English *cow-sigh*, NOT *cow's eye*. There are admittedly tendencies to voicing intervocalic *s* in the Romance languages, but these are of late origin.

In very early times intervocalic *s* had generally developed to voiced [z], but this sound was not maintained in Latin and was changed to *r* (cf. Latin genitive plural *-ārum* beside Sanskrit *-āsām* and Oscan *-azum*). Cicero helps to date this change by informing us (*Fam.* ix, 21, 2) that L. Papirius Crassus, censor in 338 B.C., was the first of his family to change his name from Papisius. In fact in all but a few cases Latin intervocalic *s* derives either from an earlier *ss* which was then simplified after long vowels and diphthongs[1] (e.g. *causa, cāsus* from earlier

---

[1] Except in the contracted perfect infinitives, *amāsse*, etc., by analogy with *amāuisse*; though even here one authority (Nisus, first century A.D.) is quoted as favouring simplification (Velius Longus, K. vii, 79).

3-2

caussa, cāssus) or from an original *initial s* (e.g. *positus* from *po-situs*); a few examples such as *miser, casa, rosa, asinus, pausa,* have various other origins and explanations.

A further indication of the voiceless nature of intervocalic Latin *s* is seen in Greek transcriptions, which invariably use σ, never ζ (which had the value [z] in the Roman period), e.g. Καισαρ; and the same is shown as late as the fourth century A.D. by the Gothic borrowing *kaisar*.

The *ss* of classical Latin is of course also to be pronounced voiceless, *and double* (cf. p. 11). In most classical texts this is found only after short vowels, since, as mentioned above, a double-*s* was simplified after long vowels or diphthongs (thus e.g. *fĭssus*, but *fīsus*). But according to Quintilian (†i, 7, 20) the simplification had not yet taken place in the time of Cicero and Vergil, who accordingly continued to write *caussae, cassus, diuissiones,* etc.; the simplification occurred, Quintilian implies, 'a little later'. The general reader may not be certain whether a particular word, printed by his editor with a single *s* after a long vowel or diphthong, did or did not originally have a double-*s*;[1] and he will therefore be best advised to read it single where the text so indicates. In any case, from 45 B.C. onwards inscriptions begin to show the simplified forms with increasing frequency; so that in pronouncing a word like *causa* with single *s* in Vergil, or even in Cicero, one is likely to be in agreement with at least the less conservative Latin speakers of the period.

Though scarcely a classical phenomenon, one other peculiarity of *s* may be noted. In early Latin, when a final *s* was preceded by a short vowel it tended to be weakened, and perhaps lost in some environments (most probably through an intermediate stage [h], a common development in a number of languages). This may be seen from its omission in early inscriptions up to the third century B.C. (e.g. *Cornelio = Corneliŏs, militare = militaris*), though towards the end of the century *s* was generally restored, having no doubt always been maintained, at least before voiceless consonants, in closely connected groups of words.

---

[1] Amongst the more common exceptions are *bāsium, caesaries, pausa.*

This weakening of *s* evidently did not go so far before vowels as to permit elision of a preceding vowel; but in early poetry it was so weak (if not actually lost) before an initial consonant that it did not 'make position', and allowed the quantity of the preceding syllable to remain light. We have numerous examples of this, e.g. in Ennius (*Ann.*, 250 Vahlen):

> *suauis homo, facundu(s), suo contentu(s), beatus*;

in Plautus (*sānŭ(s)n es, As.*, 385, etc.); in Lucilius (293 Marx):

> *tristis, difficiles sumu(s), fastidimu(s) bonorum*

(but *s* maintained in the closely connected *unus-quisque*, 563); and in Lucretius (ii, 53):

> *quid dubitas quin omni(s) sit haec rationi(s) potestas?*

The latest example is in Catullus (cxvi, 8): *tu dabi(s) supplicium.*

The practice is commented upon by Cicero (*Or.*, 161), who refers to it as 'subrusticum...olim autem politius'; he mentions that it is avoided by modern poets—though he had permitted himself the licence seven or eight times in his youthful translation of Aratus' *Phaenomena*.

It will be seen that this early treatment of final *s* is the opposite to that of final *m*; for it does not permit elision before vowels, and it does not 'make position' before consonants.

(vii) Semivowels*[1]

i The pronunciation of the *i*-consonant presents no basic problems; it is the same type of semivocalic sound as the English *y* in *yes*, etc. We should expect such a value from the fact that it is written in Latin with the same letter as the *i*-vowel,[2]

---

[1] One should not be confused by the Latin grammarians' use of the term *semiuocalis*, which does not correspond to the modern term. It is used by them, following Greek models, to refer to the 'continuant' consonants, i.e. the fricatives (*s, z, f*), liquids (*l, r*), and nasals (*n, m*)—but not the consonantal *i, u*.

[2] The distinction of writing *i, u* for vowels and *j, v* for consonants is of relatively recent origin, beginning no earlier than the fifteenth century. Latin inscriptions had used I, v for both (though the '*I* longa' was sometimes used for the *i*-consonant in imperial inscriptions, and Claudius tried to introduce a special sign ⅃ for the *u*-consonant); the forms u and J were of cursive origin. In the middle ages *v* and *j* tended to be used as initial variants: but the suggestion of a vowel/consonant distinction is first mentioned by Leonbattista Alberti in 1465, and first used by

the difference between vowel and semivowel being simply that the former stands at the nucleus* and the latter at the margin* of a syllable. The Latin *i*-consonant often derives from an Indo-European *y*, which is retained as such in various other languages (e.g. from Indo-European *yugom*: Latin *iugum*, Sanskrit *yugam*, Hittite *yugan*, English *yoke*).

There is no suggestion of any other value in the ancient writers, and it is supported by Greek transliterations with iota (e.g. Ιουλιον = *Iulium*). The close connexion between the vowel and consonant sounds of *i* in Latin is also seen in the occasional poetic interchange of their functions—e.g. on the one hand quadrisyllabic *Ĭulius* and on the other trisyllabic *abiete* (with *i*-consonant 'making position'); note also the variation between consonantal function in *iam* and vocalic function in *etiam*.

The traditional English pronunciation of the Latin *i*-consonant like the English *j* [dž] has no basis in antiquity. It probably goes back to the teaching of French schoolmasters after the Norman conquest, when this pronunciation was current in France both for Latin and for borrowings from Latin. In the thirteenth century it changed to [ž] in France, but the earlier pronunciation has survived in English borrowings from French (e.g. *just*, beside French *juste*). Latin initial *i*-consonant had normally so developed in some parts of the Romance world (cf. Italian *già*, Old French [dža], from Latin *iam*)—but there is no evidence for such developments until very late, and even in several Romance languages and dialects the original value is still preserved (cf. Spanish *yace* from Latin *iacet*). Its continued pronunciation as [y] until quite a late date is also suggested by Welsh borrowings from Latin, as *Ionawr* from *Ianuarius*.

One important peculiarity of the Latin *i*-consonant is to be noted. In the interior of a word, this sound rarely occurred

Antonio Nebrija in his *Gramática Castellana* of 1492. The distinction was subsequently proposed by G. G. Trissino in his *Epistola de le lettere nuovamente aggiunte ne la lingua italiana* (1524); its definitive adoption for Latin dates from Pierre la Ramée's *Scholae Grammaticae* (1559)—whence the new letters are sometimes known as 'lettres Ramistes'. For French it was taken up by such reformers as Ronsard, and was crystallized by the practice of Dutch printers, who were responsible for much printing of French books during the sixteenth to seventeenth centuries.

singly between vowels. Where once it had been present, it was lost prehistorically (thus Latin *trēs* beside Sanskrit *trayas*). With a few exceptions noted below, wherever a single, intervocalic *i*-consonant is written, it stands for a *double* consonant, i.e. [yy]. Thus *aio, maior, peior, Troia* stand for *aiio, maiior,* etc.[1] This is quite clear from various types of evidence. It is specifically mentioned by Quintilian and other grammarians, who also tell us that Cicero and Caesar used in fact to spell such words with *ii* († Qu. i, 4, 11; † Priscian, K. ii, 14), and it is supported by frequent inscriptional spellings (e.g. *Pompeiius, cuiIus, eiius, maiIorem*). In Italian a double consonant has been maintained in, for example, *peggio* from *peius*. Moreover, the consonant must be double in order to account for the fact that the preceding syllable is always metrically heavy; for the actual vowel is *short*—this is specifically mentioned by Ter. Maurus († K. vi, 343), and is further evident from other considerations: e.g. *maior* is connected with *măgis*, being derived from *măg-iōs*.

The fact that Latin orthography normally writes only a single *i* in such cases is hardly surprising, since it is redundant to write the double letter where, as in Latin, there is no contrast between single and double. For the avoidance of single intervocalic *i* in Latin observe that we find on the one hand trisyllabic *reicit* (*Aen.*, x, 473), which stands for *reiiicit*[2] with double consonantal *i*, giving heavy first syllable; and on the other hand contracted disyllabic *reĩce* (*Ecl.*, iii, 96), where *both* consonantal *i*'s have been lost by dissimilation before the *i* vowel[3]—what we do *not* find is dissimilation of only *one* of the consonantal *i*'s.

There are two small classes of apparent exceptions, but both

---

[1] N.B. In classical times the *i* of *Gaius* is always a vowel (*Gāĩus*); similarly *Dēĩanira, Achāĩa*, etc.

In *praeiudico*, etc., a diphthong [ai] is followed by an *i*-consonant, but this may mean the same phonetically as the [a]+double *i*-consonant of *maiior*, etc. The pronunciation of *Gnaeus, praealtus*, etc. was also probably similar, since the diphthong [ai] would here be followed by an automatic *i*-'glide'.

[2] The same applies to the occasional *coicio*, irregularly from *con+iacio*, which (as Velius Longus points out, K. vii, 54) stands for *coiiicio*; also, for example, *Pompei*, which Priscian (K. ii, 14) says was spelt by Caesar with three *i*'s.

[3] Similarly *ăis, ăit*, dissimilated from *aiiis, aiiit*, but intervocalic *ii* preserved in *aio, aiunt*=*aiio, aiiunt*; contraction is seen in Plautine *aĩbam* from *ăĩbam*, dissimilated from *aiĩbam*.

concerned with compounds of which the second element begins with consonantal *i*. In e.g. *dīiudico, trāiectus, ēiaculo, prōiectus, dēiero*, the first syllable has a long vowel, and there is no reason to think that the following *i*-consonant is double. In *biiugus, quadriiugus*, the syllables *bi-* and *-ri-* are light, so that here too the *i*-consonant must be single.[1]

The double-*y* sound is not a characteristic of English; but it should present no more difficulty than other double consonants, and a close approximation exists in such phrases as *toy yacht* or *hay-yield*.

One further peculiarity of spelling concerns compounds of *iacio*, such as *conicio* (also *in-, ad-, ab-, sub-, ob-, dis-*). With the exception of a few examples in early and late Latin, the first syllable is always heavy, which indicates that the *i* here stands for *i*-consonant plus *i*-vowel, i.e. *coniicio*, etc., not simply *i*-vowel. This value is also attested by Quintilian (i, 4, 11), though not in inscriptions; there is an excellent discussion of the whole matter by Gellius († iv, 17), who incidentally condemns the false lengthening of the vowel in such words. The reason for single writing here is probably, as in the case of *seruus*, etc. (see pp. 18f.), an unwillingness to write the same two (or more) letters successively with possible ambiguity of function.

u The *u*-consonant is related to the *u*-vowel in the same way as the *i* consonant and vowel; it is thus a [w] semivowel of the same kind as *w* in English *wet*, etc. Such a sound had also existed in early Greek, being there represented by the so-called 'digamma' (ϝ); but in Latin this sign had been taken over, as ꜰ, for the fricative [f] (originally in the digraph form ꜰʜ). For the Latin semivowel, therefore, the vowel symbol had to be used, as in the case of *i* for [y] (for which the Greek alphabet had no symbol).

The close connexion between the vowel and the consonant in Latin is seen in occasional poetic interchange of function, as,

[1] The pronunciation may in fact have been no different from that of words like *diurnus*, where the *i* would automatically induce a consonantal *i*-glide before another vowel.

for example, trisyllabic *silŭa* and disyllabic *genua* (with consonantal *u* 'making position'); in the classical period also it is regularly transcribed in Greek by ου (e.g. Οὐαλεριου = *Valerii*).

The sound often derives from an Indo-European *w*, though at the present day this has been preserved as such almost only in English (e.g. from Indo-European *wid-*: Latin *uideo*, English *wit*).

In the first century B.C. Nigidius Figulus († Gellius, x, 4, 4) evidently referred to the consonant sound, like that of the vowel, in terms of lip-protrusion, which can only indicate a bilabial, semivocalic articulation (in a discussion of the origins of language, he points out that in the words *tu* and *uos* the lips are protruded in the direction of the person addressed, whereas this is not the case in *ego* and *nos*). There is also a much-quoted anecdote of Cicero's, which tells how, when Marcus Crassus was setting out on an ill-fated expedition against the Parthians, a seller of Caunean figs was crying out '*Cauneas!*'; and Cicero comments († *Div.*, ii, 84) that it would have been well for Crassus if he had heeded the 'omen', viz. '*Caue ne eas*'; this hardly makes sense unless, as we presume, the *u* of *caue* was similar to the *u* of *Cauneas*. A parallel case is provided by Varro's etymology of *auris* from *auere* (*L.L.*, vi, 83).[1]

But in the first century A.D. we already begin to find inscriptional confusion of *u*-consonant with *b*, which had by then developed to a fricative of some kind (like the *v* of English *lover*, or, more probably, of Spanish *lavar*). By the second century the sound is specifically referred to in terms of friction by Velius Longus (K. vii, 58: 'cum aliqua adspiratione'), and this development is general in the Romance languages (French *vin*, etc.). As late as the fifth century the semivocalic [w] pronunciation evidently survived in some quarters, since Consentius observes: '*V* quoque litteram aliqui exilius ecferunt, ut cum dicunt *ueni* putes trisyllabum incipere' (K. v, 395); but in fact by this time the fricative pronunciation was so general that Priscian has to give rules about when to write *u* and when *b* (K. iii, 465).

[1] Cf. also the etymology attributed to L. Aelius Stilo (*c.* 154 to 90 B.C.) of '*pituitam*, quia *petit uitam*' (Quintilian, i, 6, 36).

However, there is no evidence for any such development before the first century A.D., and the [w] value of consonantal *u* must be assumed for the classical period.

Unlike consonantal *i*, *u* normally occurs singly between vowels, e.g. *caue*. But in the Greek words *Euander*, *Agaue*, *euoe*, the *u* represents a double [w] (as in Greek), so that although the preceding *vowel* is short, the *syllable* is heavy.

Finally, it should be noted that in *cui*, *huic*, and the interjection *hui*, the second letter is not the consonant but the vowel *u*, which forms a diphthong with the following *i*.[1] It is true that Quintilian finds *cui* and *qui* somewhat similar (†i, 7, 27), but his reference to the 'pinguem sonum' of the former suggests a back as opposed to a front vowel (cf. p. 34) as the more prominent element—and there is other evidence besides. The clearest proof is provided by the fact that elision is permitted before *huic* (but not, for example, before *uis*), and that in *alicui* the *cu* does not 'make position' for the preceding syllable, which remains light; both of these pieces of evidence indicate that the *u* must here be a vowel; similarly *huic* does not 'make position' with a preceding final consonant.

Moreover, when the Silver Latin poets treat *cui* as a disyllable, the second syllable is always short, i.e. *cŭĭ*; the monosyllabic form always has heavy quantity, but if the quantity were due to a long *i* vowel, we should expect the disyllabic form to be *cŭī*; the quantity of the monosyllabic form must therefore be due to the fact that *ui* is a diphthong. The grammarians are not very clear on the matter, but Audax does refer to *cui* in '*cui non dictus Hylas*' as 'quasi per diphthongon' (K. vii, 329, on Vergil, *G.*, iii, 6); Priscian (K. ii, 303) describes the *i* of *cui* and *huic* as 'loco consonantis', which would fit its function as the second element of a diphthong; and the difficulties of Ter. Maurus in recognizing *ui* as a diphthong (K. vi, 347–8) may arise from the fact that the other Latin diphthongs *ae*, *oe*, and dialectally *au* had by his time become monophthongs; he does, however, go so far as to compare it to a Greek diphthong.

---

[1] Also no doubt in the disyllabic *flŭitat* of Lucretius iii, 189 (Vienna MS).

(viii) h

The sound represented by this symbol in most languages, including English, is conventionally described as a 'glottal fricative'. In fact there is usually only very slight friction at the glottis—as one anonymous Latin grammarian observes with unusual acuteness:[1] '*h* conrasis paululum faucibus...exhalat' (K. *supp.* 307). More often it is simply a kind of breathy modification of the following vowel, and the grammarians commonly refer to it in such terms (e.g. Mar. Vict., K. vi, 5: '*h* quoque adspirationis notam, non litteram existimamus'). The Latin sound derives from an Indo-European *gh* (e.g. Indo-European *ghortos*: Latin *hortus*, Greek χόρτος; cf. English *garden*), and no doubt it at one time passed through a stage like the *ch* in Scottish *loch*. But there is no evidence for this stronger pronunciation in historical times.

h is basically a weak articulation, involving no independent activity of the speech-organs in the mouth, and (as we know from Cockney, for example) is liable to disappear. But where it is retained in English, as in the standard southern pronunciation, it functions as a normal consonant; before it, for example, the articles take their preconsonantal rather than prevocalic form—thus [ə]/[ðə] in *a/the harm*, as in *a/the farm*, and not [ən]/[ði] as in *an/the arm*. In Latin, however (as in Greek), *h* did not so function, as may be seen from the fact that it does not 'make position', and regularly permits elision of a preceding vowel; note also that it does not prevent contraction in *dehinc* (*Aen.*, i, 131).

In fact in colloquial Latin of the classical period and even earlier *h* was already on the way to being lost. Between two similar vowels the loss had taken place particularly early, being normal in e.g. *nēmo* from *ne-hemo* and optional in *nīl*, *mī* for *nihil*, *mihi*; it had also been generally lost by classical times in such forms as *praebeo, debeo, diribeo*, for *prae-, de-, dis-habeo*, and in more or less vulgar words, as regularly *meio* (beside Sanskrit *mehati*), *lien* (beside Sanskrit *plīhan*). The tendency to

---

[1] But perhaps fortuitously, since he is chiefly concerned to show that the written letters (in this case *H*) 'ad similitudinem uocis characteras acceperunt'!

intervocalic loss is also indicated by misuse of *h* simply to indicate hiatus, e.g. in inscr. *ahenam* as early as 186 B.C. (Sanskrit *ayas* shows that the *h* is not original); one may compare the similar function of the '*h* aspiré' in French. *h* is in fact particularly liable to weakening and loss in intervocalic position: it was, for instance, there lost at an early period in Old English, and now appears only in compounds and borrowings, such as *behind, mahogany*.

In initial position Latin *h* was more tenacious, but even here one finds omissions and misapplications by the end of the republic (e.g. inscr. *Oratia, hauet* for *Horatia, auet*). It was omitted also in words of rustic origin, as regularly *anser* (beside Sanskrit *haṃsas*) and even, according to Quintilian, in (*h*)*aedus*, (*h*)*ircus* (i, 5, 20). At Pompeii similarly, and therefore no later than 79 A.D., one finds, for example, *ic, abeto, hire* for *hic, habeto, ire*.

By the classical period in fact knowledge of where to pronounce an *h* had become a privilege of the educated classes; and attempts at correctness by other speakers were only too liable to lead to 'hypercorrect' misapplications. The point is amusingly made by Catullus in his poem about Arrius, with his '*h*insidias' and '*H*ionios'; and in the words of Nigidius Figulus (Gellius, xiii, 6, 3), 'rusticus fit sermo si aspires perperam'. The situation sometimes gave rise to uncertainty even in the orthography; *umerus*, for example, tended to acquire an unetymological *h* (cf. Sanskrit *aṃsas*), similarly (*h*)*umor*, (*h*)*umidus*; and there was controversy about (*h*)*arena*, (*h*)*arundo*, the favoured forms being apparently *harena, arundo* (cf. Velius Longus, K. vii, 69; Mar. Vict., K. vi, 21 f.; Probus, K. iv, 198). So far as intervocalic *h* is concerned, even the grammarians recognize such forms as *uemens, prendere* for *uehemens, prehendere* (indeed *prensare* is general at all times).

In the Romance languages there is no longer any sign of *h* whatever; nor is there any evidence of it in early loans to Germanic—thus English *orchard* from Old English *ort-geard*, where *ort* = Latin *hortus*.[1] But we may be sure that the writing

---

[1] Cf. Charisius, K. i, 82: '...ortus sine adspiratione dici debere Varro ait... sed consuetudo...hortos cum adspiratione usurpauit'. It is true that at the time

and pronunciation of *h* continued for a long time to be taught in the schools and cultivated in polite society—as St Augustine complains (*Conf.*, i, 18): 'uide, domine... quomodo diligenter obseruant filii hominum pacta litterarum et syllabarum accepta a prioribus locutoribus...; ut qui illa sonorum uetera placita teneat aut doceat, si contra disciplinam grammaticam sine adspiratione primae syllabae *ominem* dixit, displiceat magis hominibus quam si contra tua praecepta hominem oderit'. The actual sound will of course by that time have been unfamiliar to normal speech, and it is therefore not surprising that we find it replaced by *ch* in e.g. inscr. *michi* (395 A.D.), where *ch* probably has the value of the German '*ich*-Laut', a sound by then familiar from late Greek; inscriptions also bear witness to less sophisticated attempts in such forms as *mici, nicil.*[1]

The only safe rule for the English reader is to pronounce Latin *h* as such wherever he finds it in his modern texts (except in *humerus, humor, humidus, ahenus*, where it is certainly out of place). He will thereby be following, with perhaps even greater consistency than the native speaker, the habits of at least the most literate levels of classical Roman society.

Between vowels it is probable that *h* was subject to voicing—a tendency that is also prevalent in English (e.g. in the pronunciation of *behind*).

(ix) x and z

x and *z* are not, strictly speaking, members of the consonant system of Latin. *x* simply stands for *cs* (cf. occasional inscr. *uicsit*, etc.),[2] being ultimately derived from the western Greek alphabet in which χ had the value of Attic ξ; and *z* was adopted

---

of borrowing Germanic *h* may still have been like the modern German '*ach*-Laut' (cf. *Cherusci* in Caesar); but if the Latin aspirate had been at all evident, we should expect it to be so represented—as, for example, English *h* is represented in Russian (optionally) or Modern Greek.

[1] The name of the letter *h* (English *aitch*, from Old French *ache*; cf. Italian *acca*) probably derives from a late Latin *acc*(*h*)*a*, substituted for *ahha* (cf. Italian, Spanish *effe* for *f*, etc.).

[2] Also sometimes rendered by *cx, xs*, and even *xx*.

only in order to render the pronunciation of Greek ζ (Z).[1] By the time of this adoption (in the first century B.C.) the value of the Greek ζ was a voiced fricative [z], as in English *zeal*, and this is therefore its value in Latin.[2] Before the adoption of the foreign sound and letter, the Greek ζ had been rendered by its nearest Latin equivalent, viz. by the voiceless *s* initially and *ss* medially, e.g. *sona* (Plaut.), *Setus* (inscr.), *massa* = ζώνη, Ζῆθος, μᾶζα. The double consonant in medial position probably reflects a Greek medial value [zz], and in intervocalic position in Latin verse *z* does in fact always 'make position', and is therefore to be pronounced double,[3] e.g. *gaza, Amazon, Mezentius*. In initial position there is no reason why *z* should 'make position' in Latin, but in fact the classical poets do avoid placing it after a short final vowel (in the same way as they tend to avoid any initial groups containing *s* in this position), except in the case of *Zacynthus* (e.g. *Aen.*, iii, 270). The reason for both the avoidance and the particular exception lies in the Greek model—for in Homer, where Z had the value [dz] or [zd], such an initial group would normally 'make position'; but an exception was made for words which could not otherwise be fitted into a hexameter (as Ζάκυνθος, Ζέλεια; cf. also Σκάμανδρος, σκέπαρνον).

[1] Then also occasionally to render a σ (*s*) which was voiced before a voiced consonant, e.g. inscr. *zmaragdus, azbestus, Lezbia* (this practice is criticized by Priscian, K. ii, 42, but is in fact common in Greek inscriptions also from the fourth century B.C.); *s* does not occur before voiced consonants (except initially before semivocalic *u*, and very occasionally in compounds) in native Latin words.

[2] Several of the grammarians refer to it in terms of a combination of *s* and *d* or *d* and *s*; but this is simply taken over or modified from descriptions of the classical Greek value. The correct value, for both Latin and late Greek, is clearly indicated by Velius Longus († K. vii, 51).

[3] Cf. Probus, K. iv, 256: '*z*...quoniam duplex est, facit positione longam'.

CHAPTER 2

VOWELS

(i) Simple vowels

The basic vowel-system of Latin may be set out in the form of
a conventional vowel-diagram*. It is, however, most clearly
illustrated by treating it as two separate but related sub-systems
of long* and short* vowels respectively. As is commonly the
case, the long-vowel subsystem occupies a larger periphery of
articulation than the short, the short vowels being in general
more laxly articulated and so less far removed than the corresponding long vowels from the 'neutral' position of the speech
organs.

There appears to have been no great difference in quality
between long and short *a*, but in the case of the close* and
mid* vowels (*i* and *u*, *e* and *o*) the long appear to have been
appreciably closer than the short. The two sub-systems may be
superimposed on one another as follows:

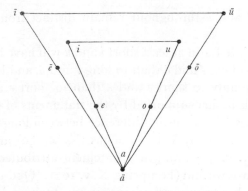

The relative height (closeness) of the long and short *i*, *u* can
be estimated with fair accuracy. In the later development of
Latin the diphthong *ae* changed to a new long mid vowel, more
open* than the long *ē*, which we may symbolize as *ę̄* (and in
some parts of the Romance world *au* similarly developed to

47

an $ǭ$, more open than $ō$). Thus the front axis now had the form:

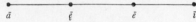

$$ā \qquad ę̄ \qquad ē \qquad ī$$

When subsequently the differences of vowel-length were lost, the formerly long $ē$ and $ō$ became merged with the formerly short i and u to give Romance $ẹ/ọ$ respectively,[1] whilst the $ę̄$ and (where applicable) $ǭ$ were merged with the formerly short e and o as Romance $ę/ǫ$ respectively; which suggests that the Latin short i/u were not far removed in quality from the long $ē/ō$, and the short e/o not far removed from the late Latin $ę̄/ǭ$. The following examples demonstrate the situation for the front-vowel axis:

Classical *uīuere*	(Romance *i*)	Italian *vivere*
Classical *pĭra* Classical *uērum*	(Romance *ẹ*)	Italian *pera, vero*
Classical *mĕl* Classical *caelum*	(Romance *ę*)	Italian *miele, cielo*
Classical *mǎre* Classical *cārum*	(Romance *a*)	Italian *mare, caro*

The long $ī$ and $ū$ throughout remain distinct from the other vowels.

Thus for late Latin at least short i and u will have been nearer in quality to long $ē$ and $ō$ than to long $ī$ and $ū$, and long $ē$ and $ō$ nearer in quality to short i and u than to short e and o. This hypothesis is in fact supported by the statements of some of the grammarians. An acoustic difference between long and short i is clearly observed by Velius Longus (K. vii, 49) and by Consentius († K. v, 394), and in a statement attributed to Terentianus Maurus we find (Pompeius, K. v, 102): 'Quotienscumque *e* longam volumus proferri, uicina sit ad *i* litteram.' In Terentianus' own work († K. vi, 329) we find a reference to the pronunciation of long $ō$ as having a greater degree of lip-rounding* (and so, we may infer, of closeness) than the short o.

---

[1] Except in Sardinian, north Corsican, some south Italian dialects, and (in the case of $ō/u$) Rumanian.

In a statement of Servius (fourth to fifth centuries A.D.: K. iv, 421), at a time when the change of *ae* to *ę̄* had taken place, we also find an indication of the value of short *e*: '*E* quando... correptum, uicinum est ad sonum diphthongi' (i.e. *ae*).

The qualitative similarity of short *i* and long *ē* is also illustrated from early times by the tendency of inscriptions to write *e* for short *i* and *i* for long *ē*, e.g. *trebibos, menus, minsis* for *tribibus, minus, mēnsis*; and by the frequent use of Greek ε to render Latin short *i*, e.g. Λεπεδος, κομετιον, Δομετιος, Τεβεριος = *Lepidus, comitium, Domitius, Tiberius*.[1] The similarity of short *u* and long *ō* is likewise illustrated by inscr. *colomnas, sob, octubris, punere* for *columnas, sub, octōbris, pōnere* (Greek o for Latin short *u* cannot be used as evidence, since Greek in any case had no short [u] sound).[2]

There were, however, as the diagram suggests, clear differences between long *ī* and long *ē*, and between short *i* and short *e*. The difference of oral aperture is exceptionally well noted by Terentianus Maurus († K. vi, 329), with special reference to the greater palatal contact of the tongue in the case of *ī* and *i*.

Similar differences of aperture apply between *ū/u* and *ō/o*, in regard to which Marius Victorinus, following Terentianus, mentions the particularly close lip-rounding of *ū/u* (K. vi, 33: '*V* litteram quotiens enuntiamus, productis et coeuntibus labris efferemus').

No particular problems are presented by the long and short *a* vowels. Their open aperture is well described by Terentianus (K. vi, 328). This is supported by the developments in the Romance languages, which also indicate the lack of qualitative difference between the long and short *a*. Similarly both vowels are represented by α in Greek.

Long *ī* and *ū* are to be pronounced rather as the vowels of *feet* and *fool* respectively (though most English speakers tend in varying degrees to diphthongize these sounds, starting with a vowel which is less than fully close). Short *i* and *u* had much

---

[1] And conversely Latin *i* for Greek ε in, for example, inscr. *Philumina* = Φιλουμένη.

[2] But the converse Latin *u* for Greek o is relevant: e.g. *purpura, gummi* = πορφύρα, κόμμι, and inscr. *empurium* = ἐμπόριον (*emporium* is due to the influence of Greek spelling).

the same value as the corresponding vowels in *pit* and *put*; and short *e* and *o* were similar to the vowels of *pet* and *pot*. Long *ē* and *ō* present rather greater difficulty for R.P.* speakers, since this dialect contains nothing really similar; the nearest are the sounds of e.g. *bait* and *boat*—but these are very distinctly diphthongs, [ei] and [ou] respectively, which the Latin vowels were not. More similar in quality to the Latin vowels are the pure vowels used for these same words in Scotland and Northumberland (but not in Yorkshire and Lancashire, where the vowel, though pure, is too open). Another close comparison of quality would be with the vowels of French *gai* and *beau*, or of German *Beet* and *Boot*.

The first and second vowels of Italian *amare* are closely similar to the sounds assumed for Latin short and long *a* respectively. The nearest English R.P. equivalent for the long vowel is the *a* of *father*, but this has really too retracted a quality (though a more forward quality is heard in some northern dialects). For the short *a* the nearest equivalent acoustically is the sound of the vowel [ʌ] in R.P. *cup*, N.B. NOT the [æ] of *cap*.

English speakers need to take special care not to reduce unstressed short vowels to the 'neutral' vowel [ə], e.g. not to pronounce the last two vowels of *aspera* or *tempora* like those of R.P. *murderer*. They need also to take care about the short vowels *e* and *o* in final position. These do not occur at the end of English words; and English speakers consequently tend to change the final *e* to short *i* in their pronunciation of e.g. *pete* (pronouncing it as English *petty*), and the final *o* to the diphthong [ou] (as in English *follow*) in their pronunciation of e.g. *modŏ*. The final vowels of these words should be pronounced in the same way as those of their first syllables; their actual pronunciation presents no difficulty for English speakers—it is simply a matter of pronouncing them in an unaccustomed position in the word.

Special qualities. In many languages close and/or mid vowels tend to be more open before *r* than in other environments; thus, in French, Villon rhymes *terme* with *arme*; in English *sterre*, *person* have become *star, parson,* and *i* and *u* have become a mid central* [ə] in *dirt, turf.* In the development of Latin also *r* had an effect on vowel quality—note, for example, *reperio* (from *pario*) beside *reficio* (from *facio*), *cineris* beside *cinis, foret* beside *fuit.* These changes are of course already accomplished facts in classical Latin; but the tendency to open short vowels before *r* seems to have continued—one finds, for example, inscr. *passar, carcaris,* and Probus notes such forms as *ansar, nouarca;* a similar tendency after *r* seems to be attested by *parantalia* (Probus),[1] less certainly in the early inscriptional *militare* for *militari(s),* and the form *here* permitted by Priscian alongside *heri,*[2] whereas he admits only *ibi, ubi* (in these latter cases, however, other explanations are possible).

It seems fairly certain, then, that at least in the case of short *e* before *r* the vowel tended to have a more open quality. But clearly it was not normally as open as *a,* and since the degree of opening is unknown, there is no point in attempting to reproduce it.

Before another vowel, on the other hand, short *e* seems to have had a closer (more *i*-like) quality than elsewhere, e.g. inscr. *mia, balnia, ariam,* Probus *solia, calcius* (and Greek transcriptions ἀρια, Κεριαλις, etc.); note also that *e* is subject to poetic synizesis in the same way as *i* (e.g. in Vergil disyllabic *alveo, aurea* as trisyllabic *abiete*). The tendency is attributed to an early period by Velius Longus (K. vii, 77: '*mium*...per *i* antiquis relinquamus'); but later also the vowel in this environment largely develops in the same way as an *i* (e.g. Spanish *dios* from *deus*). But it is evident that in careful Latin speech *e* even here was kept distinct from *i*; English speakers will automatically give a closer quality to *e* in this environment, and in so doing will probably approximate very closely to the Latin state of affairs.

The Latin short *i* also may well have had a closer quality (more like that of the long *ī*) before vowels, to judge from the

---

[1] In all these cases, however, the *a* of a neighbouring syllable may have been an accessory factor.

[2] K. iii, 71. Note also Quintilian, i, 4, 8: 'in *here* neque *e* plane neque *i* auditur'.

Romance developments of Latin *dies* (Italian/Old French *di*, as *chi/qui* from *quī*); this is indicated also by the fact that *i* is scarcely ever written as *e* in this position (cf. p. 49), and is indeed often written with the *I* longa (e.g. *prIusquam, dIes, pIus*). There is a close parallel to this situation in English, where the first vowel of e.g. *react* is closer than that of *recall*, being more similar in quality to the long *ī*; English speakers of Latin will therefore also automatically make this adjustment.

These closer pre-vocalic qualities of *e* and *i* are probably due to the *y*-'glide' which automatically follows them in these conditions[1]—and which the English speaker will automatically produce.

y This is not a member of the native Latin sound-system, but was introduced in order to render the Greek υ (Υ). In earlier times the Greek sound had been rendered, in both spelling and pronunciation, by Latin *u*. Thus, for example, Greek βύρση was adopted as Latin *bursa*, and the Latin vowel-quality is vouched for by Italian *borsa*, French *bourse*. In Plautus also we find the *u*-value suggested by a pun on the name Λυδός in (*Bacch.*, 129):

> non omnis aetas, *Lude, ludo* conuenit.

Other evidence is provided by early inscriptional writings, such as *Sibulla*, and Ennius' pronunciation of *Pyrrhus* as *Burrus* (cf. p. 13).

During the classical period, however, both the Greek sound and the letter *y* were adopted in educated circles. For both short and long vowels the sound had the [ü] quality of the French *u* in *lune* or German *ü* in *über*.[2] When, therefore, Latin borrowings from Greek are written with *y*, they are to be pronounced in this manner (thus e.g. *hymnus, Hyacinthus, symbolus, nympha,*

---

[1] There seems to have been a similar effect on *u* before a vowel (e.g. in *duo*), due to an automatic *w*-'glide'.

[2] The only native Latin sound similar to Greek υ was the *u* element of *qu* before a front vowel (see p. 17). It is therefore not surprising to find that Greek κυ is occasionally represented by Latin *qui* (thus inscr. *Quinici, Quirillus, Quiriace* for Κυνικοί, Κύριλλος, Κυριακή). At some time also the classical Latin diphthong *oe* came to have the value [ȫ], and finally [ē] (see p. 62). [ȫ] is not far removed in quality from [ü], hence the inscr. spellings *Moesia, Mesia* for Μυσία.

satyrus, mysterium, Olympia). This pronunciation, however, did not necessarily penetrate into colloquial speech; in *crypta* (from Greek κρύπτη), for example, the form *crupta* is attested by a republican inscription and further supported by Romance developments (e.g. Italian *grotta*).

In the popular Greek speech of some areas from the second or third century A.D. onwards υ had become confused with ι; consequently some borrowings into late Latin are taken over with *i* rather than *y*,[1] and the spelling of earlier loans with *i* becomes common. This development is censured by the grammarians (e.g. Probus, '*gyrus* non *girus*'), but is normal for such words in Romance (Italian *girare*, French *girer*, etc.).

As might be expected, we find a good deal of false spelling, and no doubt pronunciation, with *y* for native Latin *u*, and in the later period for native Latin *i*. Thus Charisius (K. i, 103) and Caper (K. vii, 105) both find it necessary to censure *gyla* for *gula*, and Probus insists '*crista* non *crysta*'. In many cases the false forms are probably due to the influence of real or imagined relations with Greek—thus *inclytus*,[2] *corylus* for *inclutus*, *corulus* after Greek κλυτός, κάρυον (cf. Priscian, K. ii, 36), and *myser*, *sylua* for *miser*, *silua* after Greek μυσαρός, ὕλη (cf. Macrobius, *Comm. in Somn. Scip.* i, 12, 6 f.).

Old Latin ẹ̄. Though we are not directly concerned with pre-classical phonology, some knowledge of this particular vowel is necessary for an understanding of certain peculiarities in Plautus and Terence.

In the earliest recorded forms of Latin there had existed a diphthong *ei*, seen for example in the fourth-century inscriptional forms *deiuos, nei* = classical *dīuus, nī*. In the third century this diphthong began to change into a long vowel, first at the ends of words, then elsewhere; evidence for this comes from spellings with *e*, the earliest being nominative plural *ploirume*, dative singular *dioue* (= cl. *plurimi, Ioui*) *c.* 250 B.C., followed by *uecos*

---

[1] In rural areas already occasional instances in republican inscriptions, e.g. *Sisipus*.
[2] Whence also *inclitus* (*inclutus* is normal in inscrr. up to the second century A.D.).

(= cl. *uīcus*) ? third century, and *conpromesise* (= cl. *compromisisse*)
189 B.C. The spelling with *ei*, however, also continues (e.g.
189 B.C. *inceideretis, ceiuis, deicerent*, nominative plural *uirei*), and
further evidence for the change to a monophthong is provided
by such 'reverse' spellings as *decreiuit* for *decrēuit*, which never
had had a diphthong.

The new monophthong, however, was clearly different from *ī*,
which continues to be written with *i* (e.g. *scriptum* and genitive
singular *sacri*); and it must also have been distinct from *ē*, since
the two vowels later develop differently (see below). The obvious
interpretation is that the new vowel had a quality intermediate
between *ē* and *ī*, which is usually symbolized as *ę̄* (it may be
that at this time the inherited *ē* was rather more open than in
the classical period, so that there would have been more vowel-
space to accommodate the new sound).

This was the state of affairs, then, at the period when Plautus
and Terence were writing. But subsequently, around 150 B.C.,
a further change took place, whereby the *ę̄* vowel became
merged with *ī*, as in classical Latin. The earliest inscriptional
example of this change is nominative plural *purgati* (*c.* 160 B.C.),
for earlier *purgatei/purgate*. As might be expected, spellings with
ei continued for some time (though the *e* spelling dropped out
as unnecessarily ambiguous), and the change to *ī* is equally
demonstrated by reverse writings such as *audeire, faxseis, omneis*
(= *omnīs*),[1] genitive singular *cogendei*, which had always in fact
been pronounced with *ī*.

The true state of affairs in Plautus and Terence has been
concealed by the efforts of inadequately informed editors,
ancient and modern. The texts have in fact been 'modernized',
to the extent of replacing all original *ę̄*'s by *ī* (i.e. by writing *i*
for original *ei*). Metrical evidence, however, cannot be covered
up. Thus the genitive singular of *filius* is regularly disyllabic in
their work, but the nominative plural trisyllabic; this is because
in the genitive singular the final *ī* is original and so contracted
with the preceding *ĭ*—thus *filĭī* became *filī*; but in the nominative
plural the final *ī* was formerly *ę̄*, and so did not contract—thus

---

[1] Also in MS. (A) of Plautus, *Mn.*, 237.

filiē. Conversely both poets show only *dī*, never *dĕī*, for the nominative plural of *deus*, because the original form was *dĕē̦*, which contracted to *dē̦*.[1] There is also some evidence for *īra=ē̦ra* in the pun on *īra/ĕra* in *Truc.*, 262–4 (with Spengel's emendation).

The purist reader would therefore be justified in reading the nominative plural text forms *filii*, *di* as *filiē̦*, *dē̦* respectively. But this would hardly be wise; for, unless he is also a comparative linguist, he will not know in a number of other cases when the *ī* of the text is or is not original; and in any case, since we cannot be sure of the value of inherited *ē* in the time of Plautus and Terence, we cannot be sure either of the precise value of *ē̦*— the latter might in fact well have had something like the classical value of the former. We must therefore be content to read these poets with the pronunciation that Cicero, say, might have given them.

It may be noted that in rustic Latin the *ē̦* vowel seems not to have developed to *ī*. It is probably relevant that in such dialects the original diphthong *ae* had early developed to an open mid *ē̦*—as much later in Latin generally (see p. 47); their inherited *ē*, therefore, was probably closer than in Plautine Latin, and their *ē̦* presumably merged with this. We consequently find Varro referring to the pronunciations *uĕlla* and *spĕca* (for *uīlla*, *spīca*) as a mark of 'rustici' (*R.R.*, i, 2, 14; i, 48, 2); and this is no doubt the 'broad' pronunciation referred to by Cicero (*De Or.*, iii, 12, 46): 'Quare Cotta noster, cuius tu illa lata, Sulpici, non numquam imitaris, *ut iota litteram tollas et e plenissimum dicas*, non mihi oratores antiquos sed messores uidetur imitari.' This pronunciation has in fact been preserved in some words in Romance—thus French *voisin*, Old French *estoive* from *uĕcinus*, *stĕua* (=cl. *uīcinus*, *stīua*), like *voire* from *uĕre* and unlike *vivre* from *uīuere*.

---

[1] The only *disyllabic* form found is *dīuī* (for *dē̦uē̦*).

The 'intermediate vowel'.[1] The most notable ancient source for the existence of this sound is in Quintilian, i, 4, 8, where the following passage occurs: 'Medius est quidam u et i litterae sonus; non enim sic *optimum* dicimus ut *opimum*'[2] (accepting the reading of the B group of manuscripts; as Goidanich has shown, it is common for the grammarians, in discussing any special quality of a vowel, to contrast it with the 'natural' quality of the long vowel, as here in *opīmum*).

For an understanding of the problem posed, some historical introduction is necessary.

In prehistoric times the initial stress accent of early Latin had had the effect of weakening vowels in subsequent syllables. This was particularly marked in the case of medial light syllables, i.e. non-initial, non-final syllables containing a short vowel followed by not more than one consonant. The effects of this weakening were various. In its extreme form it led to complete loss of the vowel, as in *dexter* beside Greek δεξιτερός. But more usually the vowel was simply reduced to *i*, the least prominent of all the vowels, e.g. *cecidi, obsideo, capitis* beside *cado, sedeo, caput*. Other developments are related to different phonetic environments. Thus before consonantal *u* the development was to *u*, e.g. *abluo* beside *lauo* (cf. also *concutio* beside *quatio*); similarly, before 'dark' *l* (see p. 33), e.g. *Siculus* beside Σικελός. Before *r* the development was to *e*, e.g. *peperi* beside *pario*; similarly after *i*, e.g. *societas* beside *socios*. In some cases also the vowel seems to have been affected by a kind of 'vowel-harmony', as in e.g. Finnish or Hungarian or Turkish—thus *alacer, celeber*, etc.

These varieties of development are incidentally reminiscent of certain features of Etruscan, where, for example, the name of Achilles may appear in such various forms as *aχle, aχile, aχale*.

---

[1] Amongst important discussions of this complex problem the following may be specially mentioned: P. G. Goidanich, in *Rendiconti della R. Accad. dei Lincei*, cl. di sc. mor., etc., ser. 8, v (1950), 284 ff. R. Godel, in *Cahiers Ferdinand de Saussure*, XVIII (1961), 53 ff. R. G. G. Coleman, in *Transactions of the Philological Society* (1962), pp. 80 ff.

[2] As suggested by Goidanich, another *i* is probably to be inserted between '*i*' and 'litterae', i.e. 'a sound of the letter *i* midway between *u* and *i*'.

For Latin the main point is that the vowel, where retained, was reduced to an absolute minimum of sonority, and so was liable to be influenced by even quite slight environmental factors.

In many cases the original full vowel was restored or retained by analogy with related forms, e.g. *impatiens, edoceo, admodum, integer, dedecus, consulis,* after *patiens, doceo, modum, integrum, decus, consul* (but regular development to *i* in e.g. *insipiens, ilico, consilium*).

None of the above forms presents any problem for the classical period, since, whatever the original vowel became, it remains as such thereafter. But in certain environments the vowel became an *u* in early Latin, which at a later date tended to change to *i*; the earliest example for this change is from 117 B.C., with inscr. *infimo* beside *infumum*. The environments in question are where the vowel is followed by a labial (*m, p, b,* or *f*); amongst other examples are *optumus, maxumus, septumus, tegumentum, documentum, facillume, lacruma, exaestumo, aucupium, surrupuit, manuplares, manubiae, pontufex, manufestus,* which later give *optimus, maximus,* etc.

The fact that the earlier *u* in these words changes to *i* means that it must have been different in quality from the other *u* vowels, which did not change—as in initial syllables, e.g. *numerus,* or where a medial syllable came to bear the classical Latin accent, as in *recúpero, Postúmius.*[1] In some other cases also, as a result of various factors, a vowel which might have been expected to change did not do so, having joined the inherited *u*-vowels (e.g. *possumus, uolumus, occupo*); and in some cases, although the change took place, the older *u* form came to be preferred (e.g. *documentum*).

It seems fairly certain that the sound in question must, at the earlier period, have been a more centralized, i.e. fronted, variety of *u* than the inherited short *u*. We may symbolize this as [ʉ]. It would then take only a slight shift in articulation to bring it into the orbit of the /i/ instead of the /u/ phoneme. But

---

[1] *Lubet/libet* and *clupeus/clipeus* are probably special cases, in which the *u* had a particular quality due to the environment (*l* preceding, labial following), which also has special effects elsewhere in Latin.

even after this shift, it would not be identical with the existing short *i*, and we may symbolize this stage as [ɨ]. In the normal course of events this probably soon changed further to join the existing *i*; but the persistence in writing of the older variants with *u* may well have helped to preserve the special [ɨ] pronunciation at least in some types of speech. Such a situation is perhaps described by Velius Longus when he says (K. vii, 50) that in abandoning the old pronunciation with *u* (i.e. [ʉ]), 'usque *i* littera castigauimus illam pinguitudinem, non tamen ut plene *i* litteram enuntiaremus', i.e. 'we have corrected the former broadness by (a movement in the direction of) *i*, but not so far as to pronounce it fully as *i*'.

The change of official orthography from *u* to *i* in such words is said to have been due to Caesar († Varro, cited in Cassiodor(i)us, K. vii, 150; cf. Quintilian, i, 7, 21); and Cicero is said to have considered the older pronunciation and spelling as 'rusticanum' (Velius Longus, K. vii, 49). Velius Longus (67) also mentions that Augustan inscriptions still showed *u*; but *i* is in fact regular in the *Monumentum Ancyranum*.

Opinions vary about the actual value of the 'intermediate' vowel, which we have transcribed as [ɨ]. Many scholars have identified it with the sound of Greek υ; such a value could be read into a passage of Priscian (K. ii, 7), and seems also to be implied for some earlier period by Marius Victorinus (K. vi, 20, with Schneider's conjecture): '...*proxymum* dicebant antiqui. sed nunc consuetudo paucorum hominum ita loquentium euanuit, ideoque uoces istas per *u* ⟨uel per *i*⟩ scribite'. But, on the other hand, Quintilian specifically mentions that the sound of the Greek υ did not exist in native Latin words; moreover, *y* is never used to write the 'intermediate' vowel until a late date when *y* and *i* were in any case confused; it is never transcribed as υ in Greek.

A clue to the nature of this vowel may perhaps be provided by certain other words which are said to have contained a similar sound. Thus Donatus (K. iv, 367), and following him Priscian (K. ii, 7), class it under the same title of 'media' with the vowels of e.g. *uir*, *uideo*, *uirtus*, and *quis*, where an *i* is preceded by a labial semivocalic sound. In such a case, they say, '*i* et *u* uocales...alternos inter se sonos uidentur confundere', or 'expressum sonum non habent'. We should in fact expect the environment in *uir*, etc., to have the effect of rounding the front vowel *i*: in the words of Velius Longus (K. vii, 75), '*i* scribitur et paene *u* enuntiatur'.[1] Now the Greek ʋ was a front-rounded vowel (see p. 52), but, whether long or short, was probably much nearer to long than to short Latin *i* in its closeness and tenseness of articulation. The rounded Latin *i*, on the other hand, would have the more open, lax articulation typical of the short Latin vowel—so that the result, whilst sufficiently similar to Greek ʋ to cause some confusion, would also be sufficiently different for an acute ear to notice it. Such a sound would not be so very different from the 'short' *ü* in German *fünf*, *Glück* (as opposed to *über*); even more similar perhaps would be the modern Icelandic sound which has developed out of Old Icelandic short *u*.

The English reader would be well advised not to attempt this sound. Apart from doubts regarding its precise value, it is probable that even in classical times some speakers may have replaced the 'intermediate' [ɨ] by a normal short *i*. For a later period this is probably supported by the statement of Marius Victorinus quoted above. In Romance [ɨ] gives the same result as *i* (thus *aurificem* gives Italian *orefice* as *auriculam* gives *orecchia*); and this also applies to the vowel of words like *uir* (thus French *vertu* from *uirtutem*, like *cercle* from *circulum*).

One further point requires notice; for the passage of Quintilian quoted at the beginning of this discussion continues with the words 'et in *here* neque *e* plane neque *i* auditur'. That is to say, Quintilian also assumes an 'intermediate' vowel for (the final vowel of) *here*—but this must be a different vowel-sound, intermediate between *i* and *e*, for which various explanations are possible.[2]

---

[1] In the same place it is stated that the emperor Claudius invented a special symbol (Ⱶ) for such vowels, but the passage is very corrupt, and in the only cases where the symbol is found in inscriptions it renders the Greek ʋ.

[2] It might, for instance, be a compromise between variant forms of this word, *here* and *heri*; or it might be the effect of a preceding *r* on a final short *i* (cf. p. 51).

(ii) Diphthongs

ae and **au**   These two, the most common Latin diphthongs, had much the same values as those in English *high* and *how*. *ae* was earlier written as *ai* (e.g. *aidilis*, third century B.C.), and it is regularly transcribed by Greek αι, as *au* is transcribed by Greek αυ.[1] The new spelling dates from early in the second century (e.g. *aedem* and *aiquom* on the same inscription, 186 B.C.). The change in spelling may reflect a slight 'narrowing' of the diphthong, with the vowel quality moving less far from its starting-point in *a*—in fact something very like the comparable English diphthong. The diphthongal value is vouched for by Quintilian (i, 7, 18) and later by Terentius Scaurus († K. vii, 16), who comments on the current end-point of the diphthong as *e* rather than *i*. At a still later date the diphthongal pronunciation is preserved in loans to Germanic (Old High German *keisar*) and Welsh (*praidd* from *praedium*).

In the feminine declensional endings, *ai/ae* derive from an early disyllabic form *āī*, which is sometimes preserved or archaistically revived in Plautus (but not Terence), Ennius, Lucilius, Cicero, Lucretius, and rarely in the *Aeneid* (e.g. *aulāī*, iii, 354); such forms are mocked by Martial (xi, 90, 5).

The diphthongal value of *au* is still attested by Priscian (K. ii, 38 f., 109). At an earlier period the *a* starting-point is supported (in the case of both *au* and *ae*) by the alliterative formula for the directors of the mint—'triumuiri *auro argento aere* flando feriundo'.

In rural districts, however, both *ae* and *au* developed to long simple mid vowels of *ē* and *ō* type. This we know from various contemporary references, such as Lucilius' 'Cēcilius prētor ne rusticus fiat' (1130 Marx) and Varro's mention of the form *hēdus* 'in Latio rure' (*L.L.*, v, 97). For *au* we have Festus' item, '*Orata*, genus piscis, appellatur a colore *auri*, quod rustici *orum* dicebant, ut *auriculas oriculas*'. There is also inscriptional evidence in e.g. *Cesula* = *Caesulla*, *Pola* = *Paulla* (c. 184 B.C.). In the case of the front vowel at least the result was probably an open mid

[1] Also αο, αου.

vowel of the type $\bar{e}$. Umbrian also shows evidence of a development to both open $\bar{e}$ and $\bar{o}$.

In some words the rustic forms penetrated into urban Latin (where they were represented by the standard long $\bar{e}$ and $\bar{o}$) even at quite an early period. Thus *lēuir* from Indo-European *daiwer* (the *l* is also suggestive of a rustic, ?Sabine, origin); and in the case of $\bar{o}$, e.g. *lōtus* beside *lautus*, and *pōllulum*, *ōricula* in Cicero's letters (*Fam.*, xii, 12, 2; *Qu. Fr.*, ii, 13 (15a), 4). In 'refined' speech, as one might expect, there was a good deal of 'hypercorrection', with *ae*, *au* being introduced for original $\bar{e}$, $\bar{o}$. Thus, for example, *scaena* (and inscr. *scaina*), *scaeptrum*, for *scēna*, *scēptrum* (from Greek σκηνή, σκῆπτρον)—whence further Varro's etymological *obscaenum* ('dictum ab *scaena*...quod nisi in scaena palam dici non oportet', *L.L.*, vii, 96). Similarly, *plaudo* for *plodo*; *au* cannot here be original, since otherwise the compounds would not be *explodo* but *explūdo*, etc. (as *conclūdo* from *con-claudo*). Quintilian (vi, 1, 52) specifically mentions that the old comedies used to end with an actor inviting applause with the word '*plōdite*' (though this has been edited to *plaudite* in the MSS of Plautus and Terence). And there is the story told of Vespasian by Suetonius (viii, 22) that, having been instructed by one Mestrius Florus to say *plaustra* and not *plostra*, he greeted him the next day as 'Flaurus'.

In imperial times *au* seems to have undergone a special change in unaccented syllables, whereby when the next syllable contained an *u*, the *u* of the diphthong tended to be lost—hence inscr. *Agustus* for *Augustus*, etc. This form is represented in Romance by e.g. Italian *agosto*; similarly, *ascoltare* from *auscultare* (in spite of the grammarian Caper's '*ausculta*, non *asculta*', K. vii, 108).

In late Latin the monophthongization of *ae* (i.e. reduction to a simple long vowel) became general, but the resulting vowel now was a mid open $\bar{e}$ (as already in the rustic dialects), which gives the same results as short *e* in Romance (see p. 48 above). The diphthong *au*, however, survived in parts of the Romance world, and still remains in Rumanian, south Italian and Sicilian (e.g. Sic. *tauru*), and Provençal; Portuguese shows an intermediate stage *ou*; and although French has monophthongized to *o*, the *au* diphthong must have survived long enough to cause the change of *c* to *ch* in, for example, *chose* from *causam* (like *char* from *carrum*, and unlike *cœur* from *cor* or *queue* from rustic *codam* = cl. *caudam*).

oe There are comparatively few examples of this diphthong, since early Latin *oi* had in most cases changed to *ū*; relics are seen in inscr. *comoine = communem*, *oino = unum* (186 B.C.; cf. also Old Latin *noenu*(*m*) = *nōn*, from *n*(*e*) *oinom*). *oe* does, however, survive in *poena* (beside *pūnire*), *Poenus* (beside *Pūnicus*), *moenia* (beside *mūrus*), *foedus*, *foetor*, *oboedio*, *amoenus*, *proelium* (the preceding labial may be significant in most of these); also *coetus*, *coepi*, where the diphthong has arisen from contraction (*coitus*, e.g. Ovid, *M.*, vii, 709; *cŏēpit*, Lucr. iv, 619). In *comoedia oe* represents Greek ῳ, and in *Phoebus* Greek οι (as also in *poena* from Greek ποινή, *Poenus* from Φοιν-).

The diphthongal value of *oe* is vouched for by Terentius Scaurus (K. vii, 17). The change of spelling from *oi* to *oe* no doubt had the same basis as the change from *ai* to *ae*; the pronunciation cannot have been very different from the diphthong of English *boy*. The contracted form $\widehat{proin}(de)$ presumably also contained the same or a very similar sound.

In late Latin *oe*, like *ae*, became monophthongized, but to *ē* and not *ę̄*, as is shown by the Romance developments (e.g. Italian *pena* from *poenam*, like *vero* from *uērum* and unlike *cielo* from *caelum*). An intermediate stage was no doubt [ọ̄].

In late inscriptional forms like *foetus*, *foemina*, *moestus*, for *fētus*, *fēmina*, *maestus*, we may simply be dealing with mis-spellings at a time when *oe* had become a simple vowel; but the possibility remains that they may reflect the influence of a preceding labial consonant inducing a labial (*o*) vowel-glide. The spellings *coelum* and *coena* for *caelum*, *cēna* are based on supposed derivations from Greek κοῖλον, κοινή (cf. Plutarch, *Qu. Conv.*, 726ε: τὸ...δεῖπνόν φασι κοῖνα διὰ τὴν κοινωνίαν καλεῖσθαι).

ui has already been discussed in connexion with consonantal *u* (see p. 42). No such diphthong exists in English, but it is not difficult to produce by combining a short *u* with an *i*. In *huius*, *cuius* we have not so much a diphthong as a short *u* followed by double consonantal *i* (see p. 39).

eu is confined to the forms *neu, ceu, seu*, the interjections *heu* and *heus*, the contracted *ne͡uter* (e.g. Ps.-Vergil, *Ciris*, 68), and Greek proper names and borrowings such as *Orpheus, Europa, euge, eunuchus*. There is no corresponding diphthong in English, but something similar is heard in the pronunciation of words like *ground* in some southern dialects. The sound may be produced by combining a short *e* with an *u*; what must certainly be avoided is the pronunciation [yū] as in the English *neuter*, which falsely converts the diphthong into a sequence of consonant and long vowel.

Where followed by a vowel, as in the Greek-derived *Euander, Eu(h)ius, eu(h)oe, eu* represents not a diphthong but a short *e* followed by a double consonantal *u* (cf. p. 42), N.B. NOT a long *ē* followed by a single *u*.

ei occurs only in contracted forms such as *de͡in(de)* (e.g. Ovid, *M.*, ix, 143), *de͡(h)inc* (*Aen.*, i, 131), *ante͡it* (Ovid, *M.*, xiii, 366), *re͡ice* (*Ecl.*, iii, 96), *aure͡is* (*Aen.*, i, 726), and in the fifth-declension contracted genitive and dative singular forms *re͡i*, etc. The pronunciation is then like the English diphthong in *deigned, rake, race*, etc.—though probably with a rather more open starting-point.

On *eius*, etc., see p. 39; and on Old Latin *ei* p. 53.

ou is found only in the contracted form *pro͡ut* (Horace, *Sat.*, ii, 6, 67).[1] The pronunciation, being a combination of short *o* and *u*, is something like that of the *o* in English *go*—though probably again with a more open starting-point.

---

[1] Old Latin *ou* had changed to *ū* by the end of the third century B.C.; but archaistic spellings are occasionally found in inscriptions (e.g. *ious* beside *iudicem*, 123 B.C.).

CHAPTER 3

VOWEL LENGTH

(i) General

The standard Latin orthography does not distinguish between short vowels and long. This inadequacy was not unnoticed in ancient times, and various attempts were made to render the writing more representative of speech. The first such device was to write long vowels (like long consonants) double. The institution of this as a standard practice is attributed to Accius, who had presumably adopted it from Oscan, where it is common. Thus, for example, *paastores* (132 B.C.), *leege, iuus* (81 B.C.); the inscriptional examples in fact cover roughly the period 135 to 75 B.C., except in the case of *uu*, which continues to be used, especially in the fourth-declensional forms (e.g. *lacuus*), and is occasionally found even in MSS. Except for this, the practice does not long survive the death of Accius.

At no time is *oo* found for long *ō* in pure Latin inscriptions. A Faliscan inscription has *uootum*, but since a form *aastutieis* is found at Falerii before Accius (*c.* 180 B.C.), this may be an independent Faliscan adoption.[1] The absence of *oo* may be fortuitous, but it is to be noted that *o* does not occur in the native Oscan alphabet, and so the precedent would have been lacking.

Nor does *ii* occur for long *ī*, but we know that in this case Accius recommended the writing of *ei* (†Mar. Victorinus, K. vi, 8: it will be remembered (cf. p. 54) that by this time the original diphthong *ei* had come to be identical in sound with long *ī*). This spelling continued into imperial times; but from the time of Sulla there also appears for long *ī* the '*I* longa', rising above the line of other letters, e.g. FELIcI (later, however, the use of this symbol became much extended).

About the end of the republic a new device makes its ap-

---

[1] The name Μααρκος, *Maarcus* is also found from 197 B.C., no doubt in imitation of Oscan practice.

pearance—the so-called 'apex' placed above the vowel symbol; this, however, does not appear on the vowel *i* until the second century A.D. The shape of the symbol varies, but a mark like the acute accent (′) is characteristic of the empire, and ᾽ or ᾽ of the republic.

Apart from such indications, which are not infallible and only sporadically citable, our knowledge of vowel length in Latin comes from various sources. In the case of 'open' syllables, i.e. where the vowel is followed by not more than one consonant, metre will generally provide the clue; for if such a syllable is heavy the vowel must be long, and if it is light the vowel must be short. But metre provides no help whatever in the case of closed syllables, i.e. where the vowel is followed by two or more consonants, since the metre will always show a heavy syllable in any case;[1] for this reason a long vowel in such a position is sometimes said to have 'hidden quantity', and here other evidence must be sought.

(ii) Hidden quantity

The types of evidence available (apart from inscriptional indications) may be classified as follows:

(1) specific statements by grammarians or other writers;
(2) transcriptions into Greek;
(3) considerations of historical phonology;
(4) developments in the Romance languages.

Vowels before ns, nf. In some cases one or more of the types of evidence may enable us to set up more or less general rules. One such rule concerns vowels before the groups *ns* and *nf*. For historical reasons already discussed (see p. 28), the vowel in such cases is always long; and this is clearly indicated by the frequent use of the apex and *I* longa.[2] We also find Greek

---

[1] In the case of the group plosive+liquid (see p. 89) the value of the metrical evidence varies according to period. In Plautus and Terence a light syllable implies a short preceding vowel, and a heavy syllable implies a long preceding vowel (except in compounds, such as *ab-ripio*); in dactylic poetry, however, one can only say that a light syllable implies a short preceding vowel.

[2] Even at word-junctions, as *In spectaculis, In fr(onte)*.

65

transcriptions of the type κηνσωρ, Κωνσεντια (similarly Plutarch, *Rom.*, xiv, κωνσουλας, κωνσιλιον; *Qu. Conv.*, viii, 6, μηνσα). Support also comes from a number of contemporary statements. In the case of words beginning with *con* or *in* Cicero (*Or.*, 159) comments: 'quibus in uerbis eae primae litterae sunt quae in *s*apiente atque *f*elice, *in* producte dicitur...itemque *consueuit* ...*confecit*'. Cicero's observation is also echoed by later writers (Gellius, ii, 17; iv, 17; Diomedes, K. i, 433; Servius, K. iv, 442). For present participles the same rule is stated by Probus (K. iv, 245) and Pompeius (K. v, 113: 'omne participium longam habet syllabam, ut *docens scribens*'). Probus also mentions (K. iv, 6) that the vowel is long in nouns and adjectives ending in *ns* (similarly Bede, K. vii, 230). There are also sporadic references to the length of vowel before *ns* and *nf* in other contexts.

French forms such as *enseigne*, *enfant* (from *insignia*, *infantem*) point to short initial *i*. Since, however, the colloquial language had lost *n* in these contexts (see p. 28), such words must involve a late analogical reintroduction of *ĭn* with the short vowel normal in other environments; one may similarly assume *cŏnsilium* for French *conseil* (the normal development is shown by *coûter* from *cōstare* = cl. *cōnstare*). These late Latin forms are in fact more rational than the classical, which had *both* vowel length *and* the *n*: as Cicero comments on the classical forms (*loc. cit.*), 'Consule ueritatem, reprehendet; refer ad auris, probabunt'.

Vowels before nct, nx. The same regular lengthening of vowels takes place before *nct*, and has a similar explanation. It is probable that in this environment the *c* was first reduced to a fricative [χ] (like the German *ach*-Laut),[1] and before this fricative there occurred the same loss of *n*, with nasalization and lengthening of the preceding vowel, as before the fricatives *s* and *f*. Thus, for example, *quinctos* became *quinχtos*, thence *quĩχtos*; subsequently the [χ] was lost, and since the *ĩ* was now followed by a plosive and not a fricative, the nasalization was in turn replaced by *n*—whence *quīntus*, the attested form

[1] Cf. Umbrian *rehte* = Latin *recte*.

(similarly the loan-word *spinter* from Greek σφιγκτήρ).[1] In all other cases, however, the lost *c* was restored by analogy with other forms, but with retention of the long vowel—hence e.g. *sānctus, cīnctus, fūnctus* after *sancio, cingo, fungor*; *quīnctus* was also restored after *quinque* (which by a complementary analogy lengthened its first vowel to *quīnque*), but scarcely occurs except in the derived names *Quīnctus, Quīnctius*. This lengthening is strongly supported by the inscriptional evidence, e.g. *sánctus, fúncto, cInctus, extInctos, seiúnctum, quIntus, quInque* (cf. also *Queinctius* and κοειντος). In the case of *ūnctus* the vowel length is mentioned by Gellius (ix, 6), and in *quīnque, quīntus* is indicated by the Romance developments (French *cinq*, etc., Old French *quint*).[2]

A long vowel is also found marked in *coniúnx, coniúnxit*. If, as is probable, this represents a regular phonetic development before *nx* (= *ncs*),[3] it presumably has the same causes as before *nct*.[4]

Vowels before x, ps. 'Hidden quantity' is also attested in certain morphological classes of word. Thus, for various historical reasons, in most *x*-perfects—as *uēxi* (cf. Sanskrit *avākṣam*), *rēxi, tēxi, intellēxi, neglēxi, dilēxi, trāxi, dīxi* (cf. Greek ἔδειξα), *fīxi, uīxi, conīxi, dūxi, flūxi, strūxi, lūxi*, and Old Latin *conquēxi*; similarly in *scrīpsi, nūpsi, sūmpsi, dēmpsi, prōmpsi, cōmpsi*. The vowel is probably short, however, in *coxi, flexi, nexi, pexi, plexi, amixi, conspexi, (re-* etc.), *allexi (pell-, ill-)*, also in *contempsi*. Evidence for vowel length here comes from inscriptions (*réxit, téxit, tráxi, adouxet, perdúxit, uIxit/ueixit, dIxI, scrIbsI*); from absence of syncope (*perrexi, surrexi*, beside present *pergo, surgo* from *per-rĕgo, sur-rĕgo*); and in the case of the *ē* vowels from a state-

---

[1] There is a near parallel to such a development in Germanic, but with the difference that here the nasalization is first lost, e.g. Gothic *þagkjan*, Old English *þenkan (think)*, preterite *þāhta, þōhte (thought)*, from Common Germanic *þaŋχta*.

[2] But e.g. French *point, joint, teint* indicate a late Latin *pŭnctus, iŭnctus, tĭnctus*, with analogical short vowel after the present tense forms. In late Latin also the *c* was again lost—hence e.g. *santus, cintus*; and this loss is reflected in the Romance forms.

[3] Priscian (K. ii, 466) specifies *uĭnxi*; but, like his *mănsi, trăxi (ibid.)*, this is doubtless by analogy with the present tense.

[4] But in that case the restoration of *n* must be linked with the analogical restoration of the *c*, since *s*, unlike *t*, would not cause this.

5-2

ment of Priscian (K. ii, 466: e.g. *rēxi*, *tēxi*), though the passage in question contains some invalid arguments.

In the nominative singular of nouns and adjectives the vowel is long before final *x* and *ps* if the other cases have a long vowel (thus *rēx*, *uōx*, *pāx*, *atrōx*, *felīx*, *audāx*, *tenāx*, *plēbs*, etc., as *rēgis*, *uōcis*, *plēbis*, etc.; but e.g. *nŏx*, *caelĕbs*, as *nŏctis*, *caelĭbis*, etc.). This is supported by inscriptional indications—thus *réx* (also ρηξ), *léx*, *plébs*; and, apart from sporadic references in the grammarians to length or shortness of vowel in particular instances, by the general statements of Priscian (K. ii, 323) 'ad genetiuum respicientes dicunt produci uel corripi uocales ante *x* positas in nominatiuo', and (K. ii, 326) 'corripiunt... penultimam in *ms* uel *bs* uel *ps* uel *x* desinentia, si uocalem breuem ante eas consonantes habuerint'.

Vowels before sc. Before the verbal suffix -*sc*- the vowel is long in nearly all cases (*nōsco*, *crēsco*, *pāsco*, *nāscor*, *quiēsco*, *obliuīscor*, *rubēsco*, *nancīscor*, etc.); probable exceptions are *pŏsco*, *dĭsco*, *compĕsco*, Old Latin *ĕscit*, similarly *mĭsceo*, in which the *sc* derives from originally more complex consonant-groups. The rule is implied in general by Gellius (vii, 15), and supported by inscriptional forms such as *créscéns* (also Κρησκης), *consenésceret*, *nótésceret*, *d(esc)Iscentem*, *náscerer*, *quiéscere*, *oblIuIscemur*, *erceiscunda*; absence of vowel weakening in a medial syllable also indicates *ā* for *hiasco* (which would otherwise become *hiesco*).

'Lachmann's Law.' In the course of a discussion on frequentative verbs (*actito*, *dictito*, etc.), Aulus Gellius (ix, 6; cf. xii, 3) mentions that the past participles of *ago*, *lego*, *scribo* have long vowels (*āctus*, *lēctus*, *scrīptus*), but that those of *facio*, *dīco*, *ueho*, *rapio*, *capio* have short vowels (*făctus*, *dĭctus*, *uĕctus*, *răptus*, *căptus*). In his commentary on Lucretius (i, 805), Lachmann generalized this observation into the rule 'ubi in praesente media est, participia producuntur', i.e. the vowel is lengthened in the past participle if the present stem ends in a voiced plosive (*ag*-, *leg*-, *scrīb*-, as against *fac*-, *dīc*-, *ueh*-, *rap*-, *cap*-). It is this rule that is sometimes referred to as 'Lachmann's Law'.

As such, however, it is rather too broad; and as more recently and narrowly stated by Maniet,[1] it reads as follows: '"Une voyelle brève, à l'exception de *i*, s'est allongée à la suite de l'assourdissement d'un *g* précédant", tout en admettant une certaine hésitation en ce qui concerne l'exclusion de la voyelle *i*.' Thus it is now restricted primarily to cases where the present stem ends in a voiced *velar* plosive (which is devoiced before the *t* of the past participle), and basically does not apply where the vowel is *i* (the least prominent of vowels). The rule as thus stated in fact applies to *āctus, lēctus, tēctus, rēctus, tāctus, frāctus, pāctus* (from *ago, lego, tego, rego, tango, frango, pango*), as against *făctus, iăctus, uĭctus, dŏctus, păctus, -spĕctus, amĭctus, -lĕctus, frĭctus, sĕctus, enĕctus, mĭxtus, relĭctus, cŏctus, uĕctus, trăctus, căptus, rŭptus, răptus, ăptus* (from *facio, iacio, uinco, doceo, paciscor, -spicio, amicio, -licio, frico, seco, enico, misceo, relinquo, coquo, ueho, traho, capio, rumpo, rapio, apiscor*). Further, vowel length is preserved by comparison with the present in *lūctus, sūctus* (from *lūgeo, sūgo*), but is lost in *dŭctus, dĭctus, ĭctus* (from *dūco, dīco, īco*).

As noted by Maniet, however, lengthening does not occur in *strĭctus, pĭctus, fĭctus, mĭctum* (from *stringo, pingo, fingo, mingo*), though length is preserved in *fīctus/fīxus, frīctus, -flīctus* (from *fīgo,[2] frīgo, -flīgo*). Such retention is presumably analogical, and this would also explain the long-vowel participles where the present stem ends in a voiced plosive other than *g*—as *scrīptus, nūpta, lāpsus* (from *scrībo, nūbo, lābor*). In *frūctus* (from *fruor*) the Indo-European present stem ended in a labio-velar g^w, but various analogies no doubt account for *strūctus, flūxus/*old *flūctus, uīctum* (from *struo, fluo, uīuo*), as also for *pāstus* (from *pāsco*). Long vowels are also to be noted in *ēmptus* (after *ēmi*), *sūmptus, dēmptus, prōmptus, cōmptus* (after *sūmo*, etc.).

The length of vowel in the participle also of course applies to forms derived from the participle, e.g. *lēctor, āctito*. The cause of the lengthening under (the revised) Lachmann's Law is far from certain, but vowel length is well attested, apart from

---

[1] In *Hommages à Max Niedermann* (1956), p. 237.

[2] Old Latin is in fact *fīuo*, with *u* from Indo-European g^w. But note *nīxus* (and *nīctare*) from *(co)nīueo*, where *u* is from Indo-European g^wh.

Gellius' evidence,[1] by inscriptions and by developments in the Romance languages. Thus, for example, inscr. *léctus, áctIs, infráctá, récté, téctor, lúctú, adflIctus, scrIpta, dIlápsam, fIxa, frúcto, paastores, redémpta* (and ρεδηνπτα), *consúmpta*. Romance evidence is seen in e.g. French *toit, droit* (from *tēctum, dirēctum*), as against *lit, dépit* (from *lĕctum* 'bed', *despĕctum*).

Some difficulty is presented by a number of inscriptions with *I* longa in *uIctor*, etc. But this could have been introduced merely 'ad titulum exornandum et decorandum';[2] one also finds, for example, *optImae, condIdit, Inuicto*, and especially *Imp(erator)*, where there is certainly no question of vowel length, and the purpose is presumably to enhance the quality, activity, or personality celebrated.

The Romance evidence also is troublesome in the case of *dĭctus*. Thus Italian *detto* and Old French *beneoit* (English *Bennet(t)*) indicate (*bene*)*dĭctus*; but French *dit*, Spanish *dicho* point to *dīctus*. The explanation is almost certainly that the regular form was *dĭctus*, but that an analogical form with long vowel (after *dīco, dīxi*) was also developed; this is confirmed by the fact that developments of the derived form *dictare* show only the short vowel.

There is also strong internal evidence for the long vowels arising by Lachmann's Law or otherwise. Thus compounds of *actus, tactus, fractus, pactus, lapsus, pastus* do not show the 'weakening' to *e* that would otherwise be expected in medial syllables, e.g. *contactus*, NOT *contectus* (from *con-tango → contingo*), as against *confectus, detrecto, deiectus, compectus* (from *con-paciscor*), *correptus, ineptus* (← *in-aptus*, from *apiscor*). The same evidence indicates that Lachmann's Law also applies before *s* in the subjunctive *adāxim* (from *ad-ago → adigo*), as against *effĕxim* (from *ex-facio → efficio*); it evidently did not apply to *ăxis* (cf. Charisius, K. i, 11), since the connexion with *ago* was too remote; and it is doubtful whether the *mag-* of *magnus* induced a long vowel in *maximus* (one inscriptional instance only).

---

[1] Which includes also *strŭctus*. Short vowel is specifically attested for *amplĕctor* by Priscian, K. ii, 25 (cf. Greek πλέκω).

[2] J. Christiansen, *De apicibus et I longis*, p. 36.

Note also that there is no contraction of vowels in *coactus*, as there would be if the *a* were short (as in fact in the present *cōgo* from *co-ăgo*).

The importance of Lachmann's Law and the related cases should not be underestimated. For to pronounce *actus* with a short *a* as in *factus* is no less ungrammatical than to say, for example, *redectus* with an *e* as in *refectus*. It just happens that the Latin alphabet makes a distinction between *a* and *e* but not between *ā* and *ă*—and metrical evidence does not reveal the error in such cases.

Vowels before gn. It is commonly, and mistakenly, believed that vowels in Latin are regularly long before the consonant-group *gn*. This doctrine rests upon a single passage in Priscian, which is manifestly an interpolation and misses the point that Priscian is making.[1]

Priscian (K. ii, 81) is discussing the formation of adjectives from proper (place) names ending in *-ia*, where this ending is preceded by consonants other than *n*. The adjective is formed, he says, by the suffix *-īnus*, with a long *ī* ('Si...ante *ia* aliam quam *n* habuerint consonantem, *i* longam habent ab eis deriuata ante *nus*, ut *Luceria Lucerīnus*, *Nuceria Nucerīnus*, *Placentia Placentīnus*'). He then goes on to say that the same applies in the case of *Anagnia Anagnīnus*, in spite of the preceding *n*, because, as he explains it, it is not a simple *n* but a group *gn* ('*Anagnia* quoque, quia *g* ante *n* habet, *Anagnīnus*'). There follow further straightforward examples such as *Alexandria Alexandrīnus*, and then some cases (earlier discussed at K. ii, 79) where the suffix is *-(i)tanus*. Now comes the passage in question: '*Gnus* quoque uel *gna* uel *gnum* terminantia longam habent uocalem penultimam, ut a *regno rēgnum*, a *sto stāgnum*, a *bene benīgnus*, a *male malīgnus*, *abiēgnus*, *priuīgnus*, *Pelīgnus*.' The passage is followed by a further brief discussion of proper names which do not follow previously stated rules (thus *censor Censorīnus* and not *Censoriānus* as expected from p. 78 K.).

---

[1] There is a good discussion of this passage by F. d'Ovidio in *Archivio Glottologico Italiano*, x (1886–8), 443 f.

The interpolatory nature of the '*gnus*' passage is strongly suggested by its irrelevant interruption of the discussion of proper names, more particularly those with adjectives in -*īnus*; and by the introduction of nouns into a chapter which is exclusively concerned with adjectives (from p. 68 K.—ch. VIII '*De Possessivis*'). It has clearly missed Priscian's point about *Anagnīnus*, where it is not the vowel *preceding* the *gn* that is long, but the vowel *following* it.

So far as the interpolation itself is concerned, it is important to note the words chosen for exemplification. In *regnum*, *stagnum* (from *stāre*), *abiegnus*, we might expect the vowel, on historical and phonological grounds, to be long in any case (as also in *segnis*, cf. p. 24); in the remaining examples it is difficult to judge—but whether or not the anonymous author is right in regard to these, there are various examples he does *not* quote—such as *agnus*, *magnus*, *ignis*, *dignus*, *lignum*, *ilignus*, *ignotus*, *cognatus*, etc.; and in some of these, at least, historical evidence clearly supports a *short* vowel. The change of *e* to *i* indicates a short vowel for an early period in *ignis*, *dignus*, *lignum*, *signum*, *ilignus* (cf. p. 23); and Romance evidence points to a short vowel at a later period in *dignus*, *pignus*, *pugnus*, *lignum*, *signum* (e.g. Italian *degno*, French *poing*); note also *dĭgnitas* implied by Diomedes (K. i, 470), and Greek transcriptions such as κογνιτου. It seems most probable, therefore, that what the interpolator states as a general rule is not so, and that he was at a loss to cite much more by way of example.

The inscriptional evidence is interesting. We find length indicated as expected in *régna*, etc. (also pap. *ségnis*); and on the other hand we nowhere find even so common a word as *magnus* marked with a long *a*. The only exceptional forms are *prⅠuⅠgno* (which agrees with the interpolation), *dⅠgne*, *sⅠgnum/seignum*. In all these cases the vowel concerned is an *i*, and this applies also to the doubtful examples of the interpolation. If we are not to dismiss these as simple misuses of the *I* longa, there may be some phonetic basis both for the spellings and for the interpolator's examples.

We have seen that short *e* before *gn* (= [ŋn], cf. pp. 23 ff.)

had early been closed to short *i* (as in *leg-nom → lignum*); and it is not improbable that the same phonetic environment might have continued to exert a closing influence on short *i*, thereby causing it to approach the *quality*, though not the length, of a long *ī* (cf. pp. 47 ff.). This could well explain the occasional interpretation and writing of this *i* as *ī*.[1]

If this explanation is correct, we might expect to find occasional inscriptional instances of long for short *i* (but not other vowels) before [ŋ] in other contexts, i.e. before *ng*, *nc*, *nqu* (cf. p. 27). This situation we do in fact find in imperial times, viz. *sIngulas* (*CIL*, ii, 1964), *sIng(ulos)* (x, 5654), *CIncia* (vi, 14817), *CInciae* (vi, 14821; xiv, 806). The etymology of *Cincia* is unknown, but *singuli* is certainly derived from *sĕm-* (as in *semel*) and therefore has short *i*.[2] I have found no such cases with other long vowels.

We may safely say, then, that the vowel is long in *rēgnum*, *stāgnum*, *sēgnis*, *abiēgnus*, but probably NOT before *gn* in any other instances.

Vowels before r + consonant. It is sometimes stated that in this context also vowels were lengthened. It is certainly true that in some cases the vowel was long, but it is equally clear that it was not so in most cases. Romance evidence generally points to a short vowel. Grammarians specifically mention or imply short vowels in *arceo*, *arcus*, *arma*, *ars*, *aruus*, *arx*, *parco*, *pars*, *seruus*, *uirtus* (*ārma* is in fact referred to by Pompeius, K. v, 285, as a 'barbarismus'). One finds such Greek transcriptions as πορτα, πορκος, φορτιν (from *fors*); and forms of the type *exerceo*, *inermis*, *excerpo*, *peperci* show, by their weakening of the vowel to *e*, that the *a* in *arceo*, *arma*, *carpo*, *parco* was short.

---

[1] Note also inscr. *pIgmen(tum)* (cf. p. 25).

[2] One also finds *prIncipi* (ix, 5702; xiii, 1644). On the basis of an etymology from *prīmo-caps* this is usually assumed to have a long vowel; and Romance evidence is sometimes quoted to support this (e.g. Italian *principe*). But the Romance forms are early *loans* from Latin, and therefore not citable as derivatives; and both Servius (K. iv, 426) and Pompeius (K. v, 130) in fact attest *prĭnceps*, with short *i*. This word may therefore provide a further example of vowel closure before [ŋ]. Nevertheless, the possibility is not excluded that the classical form may have had a long vowel, which was later shortened.

73

Clear exceptions are provided by *forma, ordo, ornare*, for all of which the Romance evidence points to *ō* (e.g. Italian *fórma*, with close *o*, as against *fọrte*, with open *o*); vowel length is here also attested by inscriptional *órdines*, etc., *órnátum*, etc., and *fórma* (cf. φωρμη: *fōrmula* also attested by Donatus, *In Ter. Phorm. prol.*, 26). There are a few instances of *I* longa in *firmus*, but this is contradicted by the Romance evidence (Italian *fermo*, etc.). There is strong inscriptional evidence for long vowel in *Mars* (*Mártis*, etc.), *Marcus* (*Maarcus*, Μααρκος, *MárcI*, etc.), and *quartus* (*quártus*, etc.), and there is no reason to doubt that these spellings have a phonetic basis. There are also etymological reasons for assuming long vowels in *furtum*, etc., *sursum, prorsus, rursus, larua* (trisyll. *lārua* in Plautus), *iurgare, purgare* (*iūrigandum, pūrigas* in Plautus), also perhaps in *ardeo*.

Vowels before final m. In most contexts (cf. p. 30), final *m* was reduced to a nasalization of the preceding vowel, which was at the same time lengthened. We have, nevertheless, to consider the length of the vowel in those cases where the *m* was preserved (cf. p. 31), and also in view of the fact that most English speakers are likely to pronounce the final *m* more generally, except when it is elided.

The preceding vowel is in fact always short. For *-um* this is shown in most cases by the fact that it derives from Old Latin *-om* (e.g. *sacrom → sacrum*), as *-us* derives from *-os* (cf. p. 18); such a change only affects short vowels; and even where the *o* was originally long, as in the genitive plural (cf. Greek *-ων*), it is shortened and so gives *-um*. For the other vowels shortness is attested by an express statement of Priscian (K. ii, 23): 'numquam tamen eadem *m* ante se natura longam (uocalem) patitur in eadem syllaba esse, ut *illam, artem, puppim, illum, rem*'. Short vowel is also attested for the last word by French *rien* (as *bien* from *běn(e)* and not as *rein* from *rēn*).

Miscellaneous. There are a number of other words, not falling into any of the above categories, for which long 'hidden quantity' is reasonably attested by one or more of the types of evidence cited on p. 65. The more common of these are listed below (forms already discussed are not included):

Āfricus, āstutus, ātrium, bēllua, bēstia, corōlla, delūbrum, ēbrius, ēsca, ēs ēst ēsse, etc. (from *edo*),[1] *exīstimo, fāstus, fauīlla, fēstus Fēstus, frūstra, iūstus, lātrina, lābrum* ('tub', but *lăbrum* 'lip'), *lātro* ('bark', but *lătro* 'robber'), *lībra, līctor, lūstrum* ('expiation', but *lŭstrum* 'lair'), *mālle, Mānlius, mercēnnarius, mīlle, mīluus, nārro, nōlle, nūllus, nūndinae/-um, nūntius,*[2] *ōlla, ōsculum, ōstium, pēluis, Pōllio, prīscus, pūblicus, Rōscius, rōstrum, rūsticus, sēstertius, Sēstius, stēlla, trīstis, ūllus, uāllum, uēndo, uīscera.*

It is perhaps necessary to point out that there is no evidence whatever for a long vowel in *classis*; statements to this effect are based merely on a supposed etymology from Greek κλῆσις, first proposed by Dionysius of Halicarnassus (*Ant.*, iv, 18).

The distinction *uāstus* 'waste', *uăstus* 'vast' seems also to be based solely on insufficient etymological evidence.

(iii) hic and hoc

There is a passage in *The Merry Wives of Windsor* (Act iv, scene 1) where Sir Hugh Evans is testing the Latin of his pupil William Page:

EVANS: What is he, William, that does lend articles?

WILLIAM: Articles are borrowed of the pronoun, and be thus declined: Singulariter, nominativo, *hic haec hoc.*

EVANS: Nominativo, *hig hag hog.*

After further exchanges, Mistress Quickly objects: 'You do ill to teach the child such words. He teaches him to hick and to hack, which they'll do fast enough of themselves.' Which seems to suggest that in Shakespeare's time *hic* and *hoc* were pronounced with short vowels. It so happens that this (though

---

[1] But short vowel in forms from *sum* (heavy quantity in the second person singular in Plautus is due to double consonant, *ess*).

[2] Early *nountius* (as etymologically expected from *nouentios*) according to Marius Victorinus (K. vi, 12); but Romance evidence shows later *nŭntius*. Similarly, *cŏntio* is attested by Diomedes (K. i, 433), though this may earlier have had a long vowel (from *couentio*), as also in the case of *princeps* (see p. 73). Romance evidence similarly points to *ŭndecim*, though *ū* (from *ūnus*) may well have existed in classical times.

not the pronunciation of *haec*!) was correct, in spite of the fact that nowadays these words are not infrequently pronounced with a long vowel as *hīc* and *hōc*[1] (and are even so marked in dictionaries).

These forms are derived from a prehistoric pronoun masculine *hŏ*/neuter *hŏd*[2] plus a deictic particle *ce* (cf. *ecce, cĕdo*), which gives early *hĭce* (with weakening of the short vowel before single consonant) and *hŏcce* (with assimilation of *d* to *c*). These forms are fossilized in the interrogative combinations *hici-ne, hocci-ne* in Plautus and Terence. The final *e* is then lost, giving *hĭc, hŏcc* (as in some other words of frequent occurrence, e.g. *fac, dīc, nec*).

These forms are attested inscriptionally by *hic* (also once *hec*: cf. p. 49) and *occest* (= *hocc est*). The short vowel of *hic* is clearly shown by the fact that in Plautus the word has light quantity before an initial vowel. *hocc* simplifies the double consonant before an initial consonant, and the single spelling becomes generalized even before a vowel (Aug. inscr. *hoc est*); but the consonant continued to be pronounced double before vowels, giving heavy quantity in verse at all times without exception.

In the case of *hic*, however, the *c* came to be pronounced double before vowels at quite an early period, by analogy with *hocc* (thus Ennius, Lucilius, Vergil, etc.), and this was the normal classical form (cf. also inscr. *hicc est*). The old form is occasionally still used by Vergil, with consequent light quantity (thus *Aen.*, iv, 22; vi, 791; also Tibullus, i, 10, 39).

The forms *hicc* and *hocc* are both attested by grammarians. Velius Longus (K. vii, 54) says explicitly: 'cum dicimus *hic est ille*, unum *c* scribimus et duo audimus, quod apparet in metro'; and on *Aen.*, ii, 664: 'scribendum per duo *c hocc erat alma parens*, aut confitendum quaedam aliter scribi aliter enuntiari'; for if only a single *c* were pronounced, he points out, the line would not scan since the vowel is short. Priscian (K. ii, 592) confirms the existence of the old form *hocce*, and remarks in connexion with the same passage of Vergil: 'unde *hoc* quasi duabus con-

---

[1] *hīc* is, however, correct for the adverb (earlier *heice*), and *hōc* for the ablative.
[2] For the endings compare Sanskrit *sa, tad* (Greek ὅ, τό; English *that*).

sonantibus *cc* sequentibus solent poetae producere... (iii, 6) sed scriptorum negligentia praetermisit unum *c'*.

It is therefore quite certain that *hic* and *hoc* should always be pronounced with short vowels; that when *hoc* appears before an initial vowel it should be pronounced with a double *cc*; and that except where a poet treats *hic* as a light syllable in the old manner, this also should be pronounced with *cc* before vowels. Thus, for example, Vergil, *Aen.*, vi, 129, *hŏcc opus*; *Aen.*, iv, 591, *hĭcc ait*. The heavy quantity of these words, then, is due to length of consonant and not of vowel.

CHAPTER 4

VOWEL JUNCTION

The pronunciation of a final vowel and a following initial vowel,[1] each with its syllabic value, has the Latin title of '*hiatus*'. But, as we know, this type of junction was generally avoided in Latin verse, except at strong pauses, i.e. at verse ends and infrequently at main caesurae. In prose, Quintilian (ix, 4, 33 ff.) is not opposed to occasional hiatus ('nonnumquam hiulca etiam decent faciuntque ampliora quaedam, ut "*pulchra oratione acta*"'); Cicero (*Or.*, 150, 152; cf. *Her.*, iv, 18) seems less tolerant, but his practice does not altogether support his precept.

The main problem concerns the alternative to hiatus, in which the two syllables are reduced to one. The grammarians speak of complete loss of the final syllable in such cases (e.g. †Marius Victorinus, K. vi, 66);[2] and one (Sacerdos, K. vi, 448) actually cites sequences such as *menincepto, monstrhor-* (for *mene incepto, monstrum horrendum*). The general term given to such loss is '*elisio*', corresponding to the Greek ἔκθλιψις, though the grammarians mostly refer to it as '*synaliphe*' (συναλοιφή). Such 'elision' is specifically contrasted with 'contraction' ('*episynaliphe*' or συνεκφώνησις), as in *aeripedem* for *aëripedem*.

In spite of these statements, various modern writers have refused to believe that the final vowel could be completely lost in such cases, since this would be likely to obscure the meaning. This is not altogether a valid argument; towards the end of a word sounds tend to become more 'redundant', i.e. predictable in terms of what has already been uttered; and even in the case of grammatical inflexions the sense is often inferable from other

---

[1] Under vowels we also include for this purpose diphthongs, nasalized final vowels (cf. p. 30) and aspirated initial vowels and diphthongs (cf. p. 43).

[2] The references are collated in Sturtevant and Kent, 'Elision and Hiatus in Latin Prose and Verse', *Transactions of the American Philological Association*, XLVI (1915), 129 ff.

factors in the context (it is thus very common in the Indo-European languages to find that the final syllable is phonetically weak and liable to assimilation, reduction, or loss).[1] In the first hundred lines of the *Aeneid*, for example, it has been suggested that elision could cause ambiguity in only two cases—and that neither of these 'would perceptibly alter the meaning of the passage'.[2] Moreover, Plautus (*Curc.*, 691) seems deliberately to introduce an ambiguity by this means in order to pun on *cum catello ut accubas* and *cum catella ut accubas*.

Those who find such 'elision' incredible have suggested that the final vowels were merely reduced to such an extent that they occupied no appreciable time. There is, however, no evidence for this, and it is in any case doubtful whether so minimal a pronunciation, assuming it to be feasible, would suffice to remove any presumed ambiguity.

In the case of elided short vowels there is of course a parallel in Greek; and one may compare the treatment of the definite article in French or Italian. But the elision of long vowels or diphthongs is admittedly more surprising, and Latin verse structure seems to indicate that, in spite of the grammarians' statements, elision was not invariably the rule in classical times.

Before a heavy initial syllable beginning with a vowel (long or short) there is no marked avoidance of final long vowels (including the nasalized vowels) or diphthongs; but before a light syllable beginning with a vowel, these finals are comparatively rare. An interesting study of such junctions was made by L. Brunner,[3] on the basis of data for over 53,000 hexameter lines, from Ennius to Ovid, collated by A. Siedow.[4] Out of 16,671 cases of vowel junction studied, 9871 were of

[1] Another factor in 'redundancy' is frequency of occurrence, and in the case of Latin consonants this no doubt accounts for the special phonetic weakness of final *m* and *s* (cf. pp. 30, 36), for which there are parallels also in Sanskrit.

[2] Sturtevant and Kent, pp. 137 f. Conversely note e.g. Plaut., *Amph.* 278.

[3] 'Zur Elision langer Vokale im lateinischen Vers', *Museum Helveticum*, XIII (1956), 185 ff.

[4] *De elisionis aphaeresis hiatus usu in hexametris Latinis* (Dissertation, Greifswald, 1911). Unfortunately Brunner misinterprets Siedow's category of '*mediae*' as referring to '*ambiguae*' such as *mihĭ*, *ubĭ*, *modŏ*; in fact Siedow counts the latter as short, and by the former refers to syllables ending in *m*.

final short vowels, 2981 of final long vowels and diphthongs, and 3819 of final vowels + m (i.e. nasalized vowels). But in dactylic feet, final long vowels and diphthongs follow the first syllable of the foot, as in e.g.

$$\overset{1}{imm\bar{o}}\ \overset{2}{\breve{a}}\overset{3}{ge,}$$

in only 387 cases,[1] and follow the second syllable of the foot, as in e.g.

$$\overset{1}{an}\overset{2}{ul\bar{o}}\ \overset{3}{\breve{e}questri,}$$

in only twenty cases; the figures for vowel + m are 434 and 64 respectively; whilst the corresponding figures for short vowels are 2342 and 1455.

In the *immo age* type only a small proportion involves inflexional endings other than -$\bar{\imath}$ or -$\bar{u}$; about half involve conjunctions or common adverbs, e.g. *ergo*, *certe*; and the second largest category (about 70) involves final $\bar{\imath}$; there are also a few cases of final $\bar{u}$. These facts are most readily explainable if complete elision of long-vowel inflexional endings tended to be avoided, but if inflexional $\bar{\imath}$ or $\bar{u}$ could be reduced to semivowels (= [y], [w]) by the process of 'synizesis'. Such a reduction, by forming a group with a preceding consonant, would cause the preceding syllable always to be heavy (as, for example, in Vergil's *genua labant* = [genwa], *abiete crebro* = [abyete]), and so could only be used where, as in this position in the foot, the preceding syllable was in any case heavy, as in e.g.

$$\overset{1}{pertur}\overset{2}{b\bar{a}r\bar{\imath}}\ \overset{3}{\breve{a}nimo} = [\text{-b\bar{a}rya-}], \ \overset{1}{r\bar{\imath}}\overset{2}{t\bar{u}}\ \overset{3}{\breve{o}culisque} = [\text{r\bar{\imath}two-}].[2]$$

After a light syllable, however, as in the type *anulo equestri*, such a treatment was not possible—and in fact here the junction involves a final $\bar{\imath}$ or $\bar{u}$ in only three cases, for example

$$\overset{1}{tan}\overset{2}{tul\bar{\imath}}\ \overset{3}{\breve{e}get.}$$

[1] These figures exclude the *Appendix Vergiliana* and *Ps.-Ovidiana*.
[2] This device could, of course, have been used to *create* heavy syllables before a junction, but this was apparently inadmissible (unlike the use of *internal* synizesis).

It seems therefore that the junction of a final long *ī* or *ū* with an initial vowel generally involved synizesis of the final vowel. This hypothesis, however, needs statistical checking for the position following the last syllable of a dactyl; we should expect such junctions here also to be rare.

The same data suggest that in the case of other long final vowels, the normal junction was by contraction with the following vowel; this would inevitably result in a heavy syllable, and so would be excluded from the positions following both the first and second syllables of a dactyl. In the latter case the very low number of occurrences suggests that elision was in fact avoided; the higher figures for the former case would be largely accounted for by the fact that in this position many of the words are conjunctions and common adverbs, of spondaic form (notably *ergo, quare, quando, certe, longe, immo, porro, contra*), in which no objection was felt to elision of the final vowel; there are also a number of cases involving personal pronouns, and idiomatic combinations such as *aequo animo*, where the inflexional ending of the first word can be elided without ambiguity.

Thus it would seem that true elision was basically confined to short final vowels; that final long *ī* and *ū* normally underwent synizesis (hence e.g. *odī et amo* = [ōdyet-]; *aspectū obmutuit* = [-ektwob-]; and that other final long vowels and diphthongs[1] contracted with the initial vowels and diphthongs to form single long vowels or diphthongs, though the details of this process can only be conjectured;[2] in the case of final nasalized vowels a nasalized contraction presumably resulted.[3]

---

[1] In fact only *ae* is involved.

[2] It may have involved, as one factor, a shortening of the final long vowels, as in the case of the hiatus *sub Iliŏ alto*, or (Ter.) *dĕinde* from *dē-inde* (*insulae Ionio* is, of course, not a case of shortening, but simply treatment of the second element of the diphthong as a semi-vowel).

One may gain some idea of the results of contraction from internal junctions such as *dēgo* from *dē-ago*, *cōgo* from *co(m)-ago*, *prōmo* from *prō-emo*, *mālo* from *mā(u)olo*, *coetus* from *co(m)-itus*, *deinde* from *dē-inde*, *praetor* from *prae-itor*, *praemium* from *prae-emiom*.

[3] There is a suggestion in Quintilian that nasalization had a certain hiatus value in prose (ix, 4, 40), and this is partially corroborated by e.g. *circuitus, circumeo* (but *animaduerto*). Note also, for example, Ennius *milia militum octo, dum quidem unus homo*, Horace (*Sat.*, ii, 2, 28) *cocto num adest?*

But certainly, in verse at least, there was some extension of the principle of elision to long vowels and diphthongs where metrical considerations made this unavoidable; and there was in any case no objection to elision of certain classes of words, such as conjunctions and common adverbs, and between closely connected words.[1]

On the other hand, the possibility is not excluded that synizesis and contraction may optionally have been applied also to *short* final vowels, where the rhythm did not preclude this. In Vergil (but not Ovid) there seems to be some tendency to avoid the junction of short final vowels with short initial vowels in light syllables—which would be explainable if Vergil preferred contraction to elision. Marius Victorinus (†vi, 66) seems also to envisage this possibility; for he mentions (under the term συνεκφώνησις) internal contractions of the type *Phaethon*, *aureis*, and then (under the term κρᾶσις) the comparable phenomenon at word-junctions, as in *quaecumque est*, though apparently only where the vowels are similar.

However, if the English reader chooses to apply elision in all cases of vowel junction, and thereby avoid the uncertainties inherent in other solutions, he will at any rate be no further removed from classical practice than some of the Latin grammarians were; and only very rarely will such reading lead to real ambiguity.

---

[1] For complete elision in such cases, cf. also the compounds *magnŏpere, animaduerto*, from *magnō opere, animum aduerto*.

CHAPTER 5

ACCENT*

There is little disagreement that the prehistoric accent of Latin was a stress* accent, and that this fell on the first syllable of the word. Its effects are seen in the loss or weakening of vowels in the unaccented syllables, which is typical of strong stress in some other languages (compare, for instance, English *had* with Gothic *habaida*). Thus e.g. *aetas, pergo, quindecim* from *áeuotas, pérrego, quínquedecem; conficio, confectus* from *cónfacio, cónfactus; incīdo, conclūdo* from *íncaedo, cónclaudo*. There may perhaps be a survival of this initial accent in the senarius in such forms as *făcĭlĭă, cĕcĭdĕrō*, though this is disputed.

But certainly by classical times the principles governing the position of the accent had completely changed in accordance with what is usually called the 'Penultimate Law'. By this, the accent in polysyllables falls on the penultimate if this is of heavy quantity, and on the antepenultimate (regardless of quantity) if the penultimate is light:[1] thus e.g. *con-féc-tus, con-fí-ci-o*.

Whilst these rules are quite clear, however, and unambiguously stated by the grammarians[2] (cf. †Quintilian, i, 5, 30), there is some controversy about the *nature* of the historical accent, namely whether it was one of stress (as in prehistoric Latin or modern English), or of musical pitch (as in classical Greek).

The latter view, which is held mainly by French scholars, certainly seems to have support in the statements of many of the ancient sources, e.g. Varro (cited by Sergius, K. iv, 525 ff.): 'Ab altitudine discernit accentus, cum pars uerbi aut in graue deprimitur aut sublimatur in acutum.' But on inspection it

[1] It should be remembered that in normal spoken Latin the group plosive + liquid (cf. p. 89) invariably belongs to the following syllable, so that a preceding syllable containing a short vowel is light (e.g. *té-ne-brae*, not *te-néb-rae*).

[2] The majority of the ancient observations on the Latin accent are collated by F. Schoell in *Acta Societatis Philologae Lipsiensis*, VI (1876). For a survey of modern discussions see G. C. Lepscky in *Annali della Scuola normale superiore di Pisa: Lettere*, etc., ser. ii, XXXI (1962), 199 ff.

becomes clear that the Latin terminology is translated directly from the Greek (*accentus* = προσῳδία, *acutum* = ὀξύ, *graue* = βαρύ); and more than this, in the grammarians' accounts generally the whole detailed system of Greek accentuation is taken over and applied to Latin. Except by Cicero,[1] the Greek περισπώμενον is regularly adopted, as (*circum*)*flexum*,[2] and Varro (*ibid.* 528 ff.) even includes the problematic 'middle' accent (μέση, Latin *media*). The Greek rules for the choice between acute and circumflex are also applied to Latin; thus Pompeius (K. v, 126) distinguishes *árma*: *Músa*, as e.g. Greek ἅρμα: Μοῦσα, and Priscian (K. ii, 7) distinguishes *hámīs*: *hámus*, as e.g. κώμοις: κῶμος. It is inconceivable that Latin should have developed a system of pitch accents that agreed in such minor detail with Greek, and we can only assume that the grammarians have slavishly misapplied the Greek system to the description of Latin (just as Greek grammarians continued to describe the Greek accent in terms of pitch long after it had changed to stress). The very similarity of the Latin statements to those which apply to Greek is therefore an embarrassment rather than a support to the idea of a pitch accent for Latin.

In fact not all the grammarians follow the Greek model. In Servius († K. iv, 426) we find the clear statement 'Accentus in ea syllaba est *quae plus sonat*', the significance of which is further emphasized by reference to a '*nisum uocis*' (cf. also Pompeius, K. v, 127). Such descriptions are admittedly late (from *c.* 400 A.D.), but it is likely that they go back to an earlier source.[3]

The prehistoric accent of Latin was, as we have seen, a stress accent; and the Romance developments, with their loss of unaccented vowels, point to a similar situation for late Latin (cf. *ciuitatem* → Italian *città*); already in Probus one finds, for example, '*oculus*, non *oclus*' (cf. Italian *occhio*). It seems unlikely that the prehistoric stress accent would have been replaced by a pitch accent and this quite soon again replaced by a stress accent. The absence of vowel loss as a result of the historical Latin accent is often cited as an argument against a stress accent

---

[1] Cf. Schoell, pp. 33 f.   [2] Cf. Schoell, pp. 79 ff.
[3] Cf. F. Sommer, *Kritische Erläuterungen*, p. 27.

at that period; but it should be noted that (*a*) a stress accent does not necessarily and always have this effect, (*b*) such effects may depend on the strength of the stress, and (*c*) they take time to operate (in Germanic, for example, it has been estimated that the rate of loss in final syllables is approximately one mora, i.e. a short vowel or half a long vowel, per 500 years). In any case, even during the historical period, there are in fact some such effects to be observed: e.g. pre-accentual loss in *disciplīna* (beside *discípulus*), post-accentual loss in *sinístra* (beside earlier *sinístera*), and in final syllable in *nostrās* (beside earlier *nostrātis*). Moreover, the conservatism of standard spelling may well conceal instances of syncope or lead us to ascribe them to a later period.

There is also a strong general reason for believing the Latin accent to be different in type from that of Greek. In Greek, as befits a pitch accent, its location and variety depend only upon those elements of the syllable which can carry variations of pitch (in other words, which can be 'sung'), i.e. primarily upon the vowels and diphthongs. Thus e.g. αὖλαξ is properispomenon like οὗτος, and not paroxytone like αὕτη, in spite of the fact that the final syllable is heavy, i.e. all that is relevant is that the vowel of the final syllable (α) is short; similarly δίσκος is paroxytone like ξίφος, and not properispomenon like ῥῖγος or οἶκος, in spite of the first syllable being heavy, because the vowel (ι) is short and the σ cannot carry variations of pitch. In Latin, on the other hand, it is syllabic quantity alone that is relevant; it makes no difference whether the heaviness of the syllable results from a long vowel or diphthong, or from a consonantal closure (cf. p. 89). Thus *re-líc-tus* is accented in the same way as *re-lā́-tus* (and differently from *ré-li-go*); the fact that the *c*, unlike the second part of the long *ā*, cannot carry variations of pitch is irrelevant. The contrast with the Greek system could hardly be greater, and speaks strongly in favour of a syllabic stress, rather than a vocalic pitch as in Greek. In general also (cf. p. 7) languages tend to have pitch or stress accents according to whether or not the analysis of long vowels and diphthongs into 'morae' is relevant; this is so in Greek, but not in Latin—which at least makes probable a pitch accent in Greek and a stress accent in Latin.

A further significant contrast between Latin and Greek lies in the fact that in the last two feet of the Latin hexameter poets increasingly aim at agreement between the verse ictus and the linguistic accent, whereas there is no such correlation between the Greek ictus and accent. Which suggests that there is something in common between ictus and accent in Latin, but not in Greek; and the most probable common factor is stress.

Also suggestive is the phenomenon of so-called 'iambic shortening' (or '*breuis breuians*'). In polysyllables in Latin the accent falls on a light syllable only 'faute de mieux', and in all such cases the following syllable also is light (of the type *fácilis*). The pattern of an accented light syllable immediately followed by a heavy syllable was evidently in some way uncharacteristic of Latin; and when, as in disyllables, this did in fact occur, there was a tendency to modify it by lightening the final syllable. Thus old Latin *égō, cítō, módō* became *égŏ, cítŏ, módŏ*; similarly, *bénĕ, málĕ, dúŏ* from original *bénē, málē, dúō* (whereas, for example, *lóngē, ámbō*, with heavy first syllable, are unaffected); hence also such alternative forms as *síbĭ, íbĭ*. In colloquial speech the tendency to lighten the final syllable was much more common, and is clearly seen in Plautus and Terence, e.g. imperatives *ámă, pútă*. Such a post-accentual weakening is in itself very suggestive of a stress accent; and the metrical evidence from Plautus and Terence is even more suggestive, in that the lightening may affect not simply long final vowels (which thereby become short), but also diphthongs (e.g. *nóuaĕ*) and even syllables heavy 'by position' (e.g. *uélĭnt, ádĕst, sénĕx*). In these latter cases there can hardly have been any question of 'shortening' (and so a sign ˅ has been used rather than ˘); the phenomenon is much more understandable on the basis of a reduction in the force of articulation. Such an effect would clearly be of particular relevance to a stress accent.[1]

---

[1] The 'iambic shortening' effect may, in Plautus and Terence, carry over the boundary between closely connected words, e.g. *bén(e) ĕuēnisse, quíd ăbstulisti*.

In polysyllables where more than one syllable preceded the accent, there was also probably a secondary accent (e.g. *sùspicăbar, Carthăginiénsis*: cf. E. Fraenkel,

It remains to mention certain peculiarities in the position of the Latin accent. In some words, originally accented on the penultimate, the vowel of the final syllable has been lost; and the accent then remains on what is now the final syllable. Thus, for example, *nostrās, illíc, adhúc, addúc, tantón* (from *nostrătis, illíce, adhúce, addúce, tantóne*). The same applies to contracted perfect forms in *-āt, -ít*, from *-áuit, -íuit*: e.g. (Lucr., vi, 587) *disturbāt*, inscr. *munīt*.

When an enclitic (*-que, -ue, -ne, -ce*) was added to a main word, the resulting combination formed a new word-like group, and a shift of accent was therefore to be expected in some cases: thus, for example, *uírum* but *uirúmque* (like *relínquo*). Such a shift is discussed by many of the grammarians,[1] but is then generalized into a rule that when an enclitic is added the stress always shifts to the last syllable of the main word (e.g. Varro, cited by Martianus Capella, iii, 272: '...particulas coniunctas, quarum hoc proprium est acuere partes extremas uocum quibus adiunguntur'): thus, for example, *Musáque, lvmináque*, where the accented syllable is light and would not normally receive the accent if the combination were treated like a single word. The application of this rule to light syllables is expressly discussed by Pompeius (K. v, 131); but in fact nearly all the examples quoted by the grammarians are of the type *uirúmque*— almost the only examples of the accented light syllable are the two cited above, which appear in more than one source.

It has been suggested that the general rule is in fact a grammarians' rationalization[2] (perhaps with some 'squinting' at Greek Μοῦσά τε, etc.), and that the accentuation of e.g. *Musaque* was *Músaque*. This is supported by the fact that such combinations are commonly found in the fifth foot of hexameters, where we expect agreement between ictus and accent (and similarly

---

Iktus und Akzent, pp. 351 f.), and where this fell on a light syllable it too could lead to 'iambic shortening', e.g. *àmĭcítiam, uèrĕbămini, uòlŭptătes, gùbĕrnăbunt* (cf. also Livius Andronicus, 11: *Clŭtăeméstra*).

[1] Schoell, pp. 135 ff.

[2] The same may well apply to the differences of accent said by some grammarians to distinguish such otherwise identical forms as *ítaque* 'therefore', *itá-que* 'and thus': *póne* (imperative), *pōné* (adverb): or *quále* (interrogative), *quālé* (relative).

in the fourth line of sapphics). In the case of *liminaque*, etc., the expected accentuation would be *limínaque*; but it is possible that in combinations of this pattern the accent of the main word was maintained, perhaps with a secondary accent on the enclitic; one may note the common Vergilian pattern *líminaquè laurúsque*..., etc.[1]

One cannot, however, exclude the possibility of an analogical accentuation of the type *bonắque* after the pattern of *bonúsque*, etc. Priscian specifically mentions such an analogy in the case of the fused compounds *utrắque*, *plerắque*, after *utérque*, *plerúsque* (K. ii, 181: 'communis trium uult esse generum'). But it is doubtful whether these analogies apply to the classical period.[2]

Apart from the enclitic combinations, certain other groups of closely connected words were liable to be treated as unities for accentual purposes. We know from the grammarians[3] that certain conjunctions were unaccented, e.g. *at, et, sed, igitur* (the last in fact probably arose by vowel weakening from *agitur* in expressions such as *quíd agitur?*). When followed by a noun whose case they governed, prepositions were also subordinated accentually;[4] one consequently finds inscriptional forms such as *intabulas*, written as a single word; and Plautus and Terence show evidence for enclitic accentuations of the type *apúd me*, *patér mi*. The same seems also to have applied to idiomatically as well as grammatically connected words, such as *morém gerit*, *operám dare*; but we have only partial knowledge of such phenomena, and are largely dependent on not always clear metrical evidence.[5]

---

[1] On these questions see especially C. Wagener in *Neue Philologische Rundschau* (1904), pp. 505 ff.

[2] Similar considerations apply to the trisyllabic genitive and vocative forms of words like *Valérius*, which, according to Gellius (xiii, 26, 1), were both accented in his time (second century A.D.) as *Valéri*. The same passage quotes Nigidius Figulus, in the first century B.C., as saying that this then applied only to the genitive, which was thereby differentiated from the vocative *Váleri*. But neither of these observations is supported by other writers, and there is no metrical evidence for the penultimate accentuation in Plautus or Terence.

[3] Schoell, pp. 194 ff.

[4] Schoell, pp. 177 ff.

[5] For full discussion see E. Fraenkel, *Iktus und Akzent im lateinischen Sprechvers*.

CHAPTER 6

QUANTITY

As length is a property of vowels, quantity is a property of syllables; and although there are connexions between length and quantity in Latin, the two properties are to be clearly distinguished.

When a syllable contains a long vowel, it is automatically '*heavy*', e.g. the first syllables of *pōtus, pāctus*. But when it contains a short vowel, its quantity depends upon the nature of the syllable-ending; if it ends with the vowel, the syllable is '*light*', e.g. the first syllable of *pĕ-cus*; if it ends with a consonant, the syllable is *heavy*, e.g. the first syllable of *pĕc-tus*. In order to determine whether a syllable ends in a vowel ('open' syllable) or a consonant ('closed' syllable) in Latin, it is necessary to apply the following rules:

(1) Of two or more successive consonants, at least the first belongs to the preceding syllable (i.e. the preceding syllable is closed, as in *pĕc-tus, pāc-tus*); this rule also applies, of course, to double consonants (e.g. *ăn-nus*).

(2) A single consonant between vowels belongs to the following syllable (i.e. the preceding syllable is open, as in *pĕ-cus, pō-tus*).

These rules do not necessarily mean that the division between syllables takes place at exactly these points, but they are adequate for all practical purposes.

There is one exception to rule (1) above. If a plosive consonant (*p, t, c, b, d, g*) is followed by a liquid (*r, l*), either the group may be divided, like any other group, between the preceding and following syllables (thus, for example, *păt-ris*, giving a heavy first syllable), or it may go as a whole with the following syllable (thus *pă-tris*, giving a light first syllable). In spoken Latin, and in early Latin verse, the latter type of syllable division was regular; but in dactylic verse (and even apparently in Ciceronian clausulae)[1] the former type was also introduced

---

[1] According to Zielinski, *Philologus*, supp. ix, pp. 761 f.

in imitation of Greek models. Thus in Plautus and Terence the first syllable of, for example, *lŭcrum* is always light (i.e. *lŭ-crum*), but already in Ennius we find the first syllable of *nĭgrum* scanned heavy (i.e. *nĭg-rum*); in Vergil one finds both *pă-tris* and *păt-rem* following one another in the same verse (*Aen.*, ii, 663).[1]

It is of interest to note that such forms as *uolŭc-res*, *perăg-ro*, *latĕb-ras*, *manĭp-lis* (with heavy second syllable) are admitted even at the end of a hexameter line, where agreement is usually sought between the verse rhythm and the spoken accent; yet this involves a verse stress *uolúcres* as against a normal spoken *uólucres* (i.e. *uolŭ-cres*, with light second syllable). The point is noted by Quintilian (i, 5, 28), who comments: 'euenit ut metri quoque condicio mutet accentum...nam *"uolucres"* media acuta legam'. But, as the grammarians clearly tell us (Schoell, pp. 113 ff.), the normal spoken Latin remained *uólucres*; thus Servius (on *Aen.*, i, 384, '...*Libyae deserta peragro*'), '*per* habet accentum...; muta enim et liquida quotiens ponuntur metrum iuuant, non accentum'.

In inscriptions which mark syllabic division the pronunciation is indicated by such spellings as *pa.tri*, *pu.blicia* (as against, for example, *ip.se*, *cae.les.ti*).

At all times, when a group plosive + liquid is grammatically divided between two parts of a compound word, the group is also divided phonetically, the plosive going with the preceding syllable, which is thus always heavy (so, for example, even in Plautus and Terence *ab-lego*, *ab-ripio*).

[1] It is sometimes stated that a syllable may be light before the group *f* + liquid. But there is no evidence for this as a general rule; the statement no doubt derives from the Latin grammarians, who equated *f* with the Greek φ, losing sight of the fact that the classical Greek φ was a plosive and not, like the Latin *f*, a fricative. Since *f* is the only non-plosive which can be followed by a liquid, some of the grammarians simply state that a syllable has 'common' or 'doubtful' quantity before any consonant + liquid (thus Max. Victorinus, K. vi, 242; Bede, K. vii, 230). There are no grounds for indicating syllabic divisions *va-fri*, *cini-flones* (as Postgate, *Prosodia Latina*, p. 7). In compounds, however, where both *f* and the liquid belong grammatically to the second element (e.g. *refringo*, *refreno*, *reflecto*, *refluo*) the syllabic division may be, and usually is, *re-fringo*, etc., with consequently light first syllable. In fact when the grammarians seek to justify their statements about *f* + liquid they invariably quote cases where the group belongs to a following word (thus Sergius, K. iv, 478; Cledonius, K. v, 29; Pompeius, K. v, 116; Consentius, K. v, 399; Max. Victorinus, K. vi, 217); Bede (*loc. cit.*) points out that such examples are invalid.

In itself Latin 'quantity' is simply a measure of syllabic structure; a light syllable is one which ends in a short vowel, and a heavy syllable is one which ends in a long vowel (or diphthong) or a consonant. From a phonetic point of view heavy syllables were of longer duration and so more apt to receive stress (it is in fact the heavy syllables which primarily qualify for accentuation and verse-ictus in Latin). This aptitude may be explained on the grounds that stress involves an increased contraction of the expiratory muscles, and the arrest of this movement demands either an extended duration of the vowel or a consonantal closure.[1]

The reader should be warned that even in some current standard works there is considerable confusion between syllabic quantity and vowel length—a confusion for which the Greek grammarians are ultimately responsible. In India, many centuries B.C., grammarians and phoneticians had realized the nature of this distinction, and had reserved the terms 'long' and 'short' for vowels, and 'heavy' and 'light' for syllables. But the Greeks, who were comparatively poor linguists, failed to observe such a distinction, applying the terms 'long' and 'short' to both vowels and syllables, and so came to assume that only a syllable containing a long vowel could be 'naturally' (φύσει) long (i.e. heavy); since, however, some syllables containing short vowels were also heavy ('long' in Greek terminology), they were considered as being long only 'θέσει', which could mean either 'by convention' or 'by reason of position' (i.e. of vowel before consonant group).[2] This terminology is

---

[1] This could also explain why in Plautus and Terence words such as *facilius*, *sequimini* are found with the accent on the first syllable (as in prehistoric Latin: see p. 83); for the second (light) syllable could then act as the arresting element and the two syllables could thus form an accentual unity, i.e. *facílius*, etc. (for a parallel cf. J. Kurylowicz, 'Latin and Germanic Metre', *English and Germanic Studies*, II (1949), 34 ff., reprinted in *Esquisses Linguistiques*, 294 ff.). Even in early dactylic verse we find two such syllables treated as equivalent to a heavy syllable at the beginning of a foot (Ennius *cápitibus*, inscr. *facília*). This is distinct from the regular equation of 1 heavy = 2 light in the *second* half of the foot, which has a quite different basis taken over from Greek phonology, where, on accentual grounds, long vowels and diphthongs are divisible into two '*morae*'.

[2] The sense 'by convention' cannot be definitely established before the late commentaries on the grammar of Dionysius Thrax.

translated into Latin by *naturā* (φύσει) and *positu* or *positione* (θέσει). Subsequently, in the Middle Ages or perhaps earlier, the confusion became worse confounded by assuming that instead of *syllables being* 'long by position', the short *vowel* actually *became* 'long by position'; and this nonsensical doctrine persisted through the Renaissance even up to the present day. The need for employing an unambiguous terminology, which clearly distinguishes syllabic quantity from vowel length, cannot be too strongly emphasized.

The fact is that vowels may be long or short, and syllables may be heavy or light; a long vowel always entails a heavy syllable; but a heavy syllable may contain either a long or a short vowel. There is no question whatever of short vowels 'becoming' long.

Accent and quantity in classical Latin verse

In the last two feet of a dactylic hexameter Latin poets increasingly succeeded in achieving agreement between the normal spoken accent and the rhythm of the verse. But elsewhere there were frequent clashes between these two requirements: thus in a line such as

índe tóro páter Aenéas síc órsus ab álto,

where the acute accents indicate the normal spoken stresses and the underlines indicate the beat of the verse-rhythm, there will be seen to be considerable conflict in the first part of the verse (in fact in Vergil conflict is more than one-and-a-half times as frequent as agreement).

The reader is then faced with the problem of deciding whether, in case of conflict, to allow the natural (prose) rhythm or the metrical rhythm to predominate. The latter practice has been unfashionable since the time of Bentley—but it is not altogether certain that Bentley was right in condemning it.[1] It is true that a metrical reading tends to distort the natural rhythm of speech, and is itself monotonous—but the natural

[1] R. Bentley, *De metris Terentianis* (1726), p. xvii (in *Publii Terentiani Afri Comoediae*).

rhythm would be present in the mind of the native speaker and would provide the norm against which the tensions of the verse were measured. Without some such tension verse lacks force and interest. If the verse were read as prose, there could of course also be tension between this reading and a mental image of the strict verse-rhythm. The only difficulty then is to see how the native reader (without theoretical metrical instruction) could build up any such image when the verse itself does its best to conceal it.[1] It is, however, possible that such an image could be constructed in the hexameter by extrapolation from the final two feet, where natural stress and verse rhythm tend towards 100 % agreement for both a dactylic and a spondaic foot. Undoubtedly, as L. P. Wilkinson says,[2] 'The Romans felt ...the ubiquitous desire that the basis of a verse should emerge clearly at the end', and it may be that they felt such a coda to be adequate in establishing the basis of the whole.

In the presence of these uncertainties it seems inadvisable to dogmatize for one alternative or the other—and the choice must probably remain, as it may always have been, a matter of individual taste.

Some writers have avoided the problem by denying that Latin verse has any inherent stress or beat ('ictus'), and assuming that the rhythm is a matter solely of time-ratios, which need not interfere with the stress-pattern of speech—the hypothesis of 'the delicate ear of the ancients', as one critic has called it.[3] But there are various difficulties inherent in this view. In general it seems doubtful whether a language in which stress was related to duration would have maintained a purely temporal verse-rhythm without any beat; and in particular it is hard to see why poets should have sought agreement in the coda of the verse if verse-rhythm and stress were quite unrelated factors. Moreover, if only duration is relevant to classical verse,

---

[1] In *Golden Latin Artistry*, p. 93, L. P. Wilkinson writes, 'It is only when the opening lines do not make clear what metre is being used, or when the metre gets lost in a continued orgy of exceptions, that the pulse is felt no more and the inward ear gives up'—the difficulty is that Latin verse does just this!

[2] *Golden Latin Artistry*, p. 121.

[3] R. H. Stetson, *Bases of Phonology*, p. 71.

there would be nothing to distinguish the first from the second heavy syllable of a spondaic foot, and so there seems no reason why only the second syllable, and not the first also, may be resolved into two light syllables. These difficulties do not arise if we assume the first syllable of the foot to have received a stress (at least in the 'ideal' pattern)—which was appropriate primarily to heavy syllables and so would not permit the substitution of two light.[1]

[1] The rule is of course taken over from Greek verse (cf. p. 91 n.); but the same principle applies there also, and in any case Latin would hardly have adopted the Greek model if it had been entirely inappropriate to Latin.

APPENDIX A

1. Selected quotations from the Latin grammarians and other writers

Ter. Maurus, K. vi, 331 (see p. 13).

at portio dentes quotiens suprema linguae
pulsauerit imos modiceque curua summos,
tunc *d* sonitum perficit explicatque uocem.
t, qua superis dentibus intima est origo,
summa satis est ad sonitum ferire lingua.

Mar. Vict., K. vi, 34 (see p. 16). quarum utramque exprimi faucibus, alteram distento, alteram producto rictu manifestum est.

Vel. Longus, K. vii, 58 (see p. 17). *u* litteram digamma esse interdum non tantum in his debemus animaduertere, in quibus sonat cum aliqua adspiratione, ut in *ualente* et *uitulo* et *primitiuo* et *genetiuo,* sed etiam in his in quibus cum *q* confusa haec littera est, ut in eo quod est *quis.*

Priscian, K. ii, 7 (see p. 17). *u* autem, quamuis contractum, eundem tamen (hoc est *y*) sonum habet, inter *q* et *e* uel *i* uel *ae* diphthongum positum, ut *que, quis, quae,* nec non inter *g* et easdem uocales, cum in una syllaba sic inuenitur, ut *pingue, sanguis, linguae.*

Mar. Vict., K. vi, 33 (see p. 21). *b* et *p*...dispari inter se oris officio exprimuntur. nam prima exploso e mediis labiis sono, sequens compresso ore uelut introrsum attracto uocis ictu explicatur. *c* etiam et *g*...sono proximae oris molimine nisuque dissentiunt...*g* uim prioris pari linguae habitu palato suggerens lenius reddit.

Cicero, *Or.*, 160 (see p. 26). quin ego ipse, cum scirem ita maiores locutos ut nusquam nisi in uocali aspiratione uterentur, loquebar sic ut *pulcros, Cetegos, triumpos, Cartaginem* dicerem; aliquando, idque sero, conuicio aurium cum extorta mihi ueritas esset, usum loquendi populo concessi, scientiam mihi reseruaui. *Orciuios* tamen et *Matones, Otones, Caepiones, sepulcra, coronas, lacrimas* dicimus, quia per aurium iudicium licet.

Mar. Vict., K. vi, 21 (see p. 26). uideo uos saepe et *orco* et *Vulcano* h litteram relinquere, et credo uos antiquitatem sequi ...item *corona ancora sepulcrum*, sic et quae h in adspiratione desiderant, ut *brachium cohors harena pulcher*. sed ea quatenus debeatis obseruare, ignoratis.

Priscian, K. ii, 30 (see p. 28). in eiusmodi Graeci et Accius noster bina *g* scribunt (sc. *aggulus, aggens, iggerunt*), alii *n* et *g*, quod in hoc ueritatem uidere facile non est. similiter *agceps, agcora*.

Gellius, xix, 14, 7 (see p. 28). inter litteram *n* et *g* est alia uis, ut in nomine *anguis* et *angari* et *ancorae* et *increpat* et *incurrit* et *ingenuus*. In omnibus his non uerum *n*, sed adulterinum ponitur. nam *n* non esse lingua indicio est; nam si ea littera esset, lingua palatum tangeret.

Vel. Longus, K. vii, 54 (see p. 30). nam quibusdam litteris deficimus, quas tamen sonus enuntiationis arcessit, ut cum dicimus *uirtutem* et *uirum fortem consulem Scipionem*, peruenisse fere ad aures peregrinam litteram inuenies.

Quintilian, ix, 4, 40 (see p. 31). atqui eadem illa littera (sc. *m*), quotiens ultima est et uocalem uerbi sequentis ita contingit ut in eam transire possit, etiamsi scribitur, tamen parum exprimitur, ut *multum ille* et *quantum erat*, adeo ut paene cuiusdam nouae litterae sonum reddat. neque enim eximitur, sed obscuratur.

Vel. Longus, K. vii, 54 (see p. 31). ita sane se habet non numquam forma enuntiandi, ut litterae in ipsa scriptione positae non audiantur enuntiatae. sic enim cum dicitur *illum ego* et *omnium optimum, illum* et *omnium* aeque *m* terminat nec tamen in enuntiatione apparet.

Lucilius, 377 Marx (see p. 32).

> *r*: non multum est, hoc cacosyntheton atque canina
> si lingua dico; nihil ad me, nomen enim illi est.

Mar. Vict., K. vi, 34 (see p. 32). sequetur *r*, quae uibrato... linguae fastigio fragorem tremulis ictibus reddit.

Priscian, K. ii, 29 (see p. 34). *l* triplicem, ut Plinio uidetur, sonum habet: exilem, quando geminatur secundo loco posita, ut *ille, Metellus*; plenum, quando finit nomina uel syllabas et quando aliquam habet ante se in eadem syllaba consonantem, ut *sol, silua, flauus, clarus*; medium in aliis, ut *lectum, lectus*.

Quintilian, xii, 10, 29 (see p. 34). nam et illa, quae est sexta nostrarum, paene non humana uoce uel omnino non uoce potius inter discrimina dentium efflanda est.

Quintilian, i, 7, 20 (see p. 36). quid quod Ciceronis temporibus paulumque infra, fere quotiens *s* littera media uocalium longarum uel subiecta longis esset, geminabatur, ut *caussae, cassus, diuissiones*? quomodo et ipsum et Vergilium quoque scripsisse manus eorum docent.

Quintilian, i, 4, 11 (see p. 39). sciat enim Ciceroni placuisse *aiio Maiiam*que geminata *i* scribere.

Priscian, K. ii, 13 f. (see p. 39). et *i* quidem...pro duplici accipitur consonante...quando in medio dictionis ab eo incipit syllaba post uocalem ante se positam subsequente quoque uocali in eadem syllaba, ut *maius, peius, eius*, in quo loco antiqui solebant geminare eandem *i* litteram et *maiius, peiius, eiius* scribere.

Ter. Maurus, K. vi, 343 (see p. 39).
 i media cum conlocatur hinc et hinc uocalium,
 Troia siue *Maia* dicas, *peior* aut *ieiunium*,
 nominum primas uidemus esse uocales breues,
 i tamen sola sequente duplum habere temporis.

Gellius, iv, 17 (see p. 40). *obiciebat o* littera producta multos legere audio, idque eo facere dicunt ut ratio numeri salua sit... *subicit u* littera longa legunt...sed neque *ob* neque *sub* praepositio producendi habet naturam, neque item *con*.... in his autem quae supra posui et metrum esse integrum potest et praepositiones istae possunt non barbare protendi; secunda enim littera in his uerbis per duo *i*, non per unum scribenda

est. nam uerbum ipsum, cui supradictae particulae prae-
positae sunt, non est *icio* sed *iacio*.

Gellius, x, 4, 4 (see p. 41). '*uos*', inquit, 'cum dicimus, motu
quodam oris conueniente cum ipsius uerbi demonstratione
utimur et labeas sensim primores emouemus ac spiritum atque
animam porro uersum et ad eos quibuscum sermocinamur
intendimus. at contra cum dicimus *nos*, neque profuso inten-
toque flatu uocis neque proiectis labris pronuntiamus. hoc
idem fit et in eo quod dicimus *tu*, *ego*...ita in his uocibus quasi
gestus quidam oris et spiritus naturalis est.'

Cicero, *Div.*, ii, 84 (see p. 41). cum M. Crassus exercitum
Brundisi imponeret, quidam in portu caricas Cauno aduectas
uendens 'Cauneas' clamitabat. dicamus, si placet, monitum
ab eo Crassum 'caueret ne iret'; non fuisse periturum, si omini
paruisset.

Quintilian, i, 7, 27 (see p. 42). illud nunc melius, quod *cui*
tribus quas praeposui litteris enotamus; in quo pueris nobis ad
pinguem sane sonum *qu* et *oi* utebantur, tantum ut ab illo *qui*
distingueretur.

Vel. Longus, K. vii, 51 (see p. 46). non idem est *z* et *sd*, sic
quo modo non est σίγμα καὶ δ et ζ...scribe enim per unum ζ
et consule aurem: non erit ἀζηχής quo modo ἀδσηχής, sed
geminata eadem ἀζζηχής quo modo ἀσσηχής. et plane siquid
superuenerit me dicente sonum huius litterae, inuenies eundem
tenorem a quo coeperit.

Consentius, K. v, 394 (see p. 48). mihi tamen uidetur (sc. *i*)
quando producta est, plenior uel acutior esse; quando autem
breuis est, medium sonum (sc. inter *e* et *i*) exhibere debet.

Ter. Maurus, K. vi, 329 (see p. 48).
      igitur sonitum reddere cum uoles minori,
      retrorsus adactam modice teneto linguam,
      rictu neque magno sat erit patere labra.
      at longior alto tragicum sub oris antro
      molita rotundis acuit sonum labellis.

Ter. Maurus, K. vi, 329 (see p. 49).

    e quae sequitur uocula dissona est priori (sc. *a*),
quia deprimit altum modico tenore rictum
et lingua remotos premit hinc et hinc molares.
i porrigit ictum genuinos prope ad ipsos
minimumque renidet supero tenus labello.

Cassiodor(i)us, K. vii, 150 (see p. 58). *lacrumae* an *lacrimae*, *maxumus* an *maximus*, et siqua similia sunt, quo modo scribi debeant, quaesitum est. Terentius Varro tradidit Caesarem per *i* eius modi uerba solitum esse enuntiare et scribere: inde propter auctoritatem tanti uiri consuetudinem factam.

Ter. Scaurus, K. vii, 16 (see p. 60). *a* igitur littera praeposita est *u* et *e* litteris, *ae, au*. . .apud antiquos *i* littera pro ea scribebatur. . .ut *pictai uestis*. . .sed magis in illis *e* nouissima sonat.

Mar. Vict., K. vi, 8 (see p. 64). Accius, cum longa syllaba scribenda esset, duas uocales ponebat, praeterquam quae in *i* litteram incideret: hanc enim per *e* et *i* scribebat.

Mar. Vict., K. vi, 66 (see p. 78). συναλοιφή est, cum inter duas loquellas duarum uocalium concursus alteram elidit. . . nec tamen putaueris quamlibet de duabus eximi posse: illa enim quae superuenit priorem semper excludet.

Mar. Vict., K. vi, 66 f. (see p. 82). συνεκφώνησις uero, cum duae uocales in unam syllabam coguntur. . .ut cum *Phaethon* in metro sic enuntiatur, ut ex trisyllabo nomine disyllabum faciat. . . .

    . . .κρᾶσιν, id est cum unius litterae uocalis in duas syllabas fit communio, ut *audire est operae*. . .*quaecumque est fortuna*. . . quae ueluti per contrarium συνεκφώνησιν in metris imitatur.

Quintilian, i, 5, 30 (see p. 83). namque in omni uoce acuta intra numerum trium syllabarum continetur, siue eae sunt in uerbo solae siue ultimae, et in iis aut proxima extremae aut ab ea tertia. trium porro, de quibus loquor, media longa aut acuta aut flexa erit; eodem loco breuis utique grauem habebit sonum, ideoque positam ante se id est ab ultima tertium acuet.

Servius, K. iv, 426 (see p. 84). accentus in ea syllaba est, quae plus sonat. quam rem deprehendimus, si fingamus nos aliquem longe positum clamare. inuenimus enim naturali ratione illam syllabam plus sonare, quae retinet accentum, atque usque eodem nisum uocis ascendere.

2. Chronology of sources

Accius	b. 170 B.C.
Audax	? 6th cent. A.D.
Augustine	354 to 430 A.D.
Bede	673 to 735 A.D.
Caesar	100 to 44 B.C.
Caper	2nd cent. A.D.
Cassiodor(i)us	c. 490 to 585 A.D.
Charisius	4th cent. A.D.
Cicero	106 to 43 B.C.
Cledonius	5th cent. A.D.
Consentius	5th cent. A.D.
Cornutus	1st cent. A.D.
Diomedes	4th cent. A.D.
Dionysius of Halicarnassus	1st cent. B.C.
Donatus	4th cent. A.D.
Festus	? 2nd cent. A.D.
Gellius (Aulus)	2nd cent. A.D.
Lucilius	c. 180 to 102 B.C.
Macrobius	4th–5th cent. A.D.
Marius Victorinus	4th cent. A.D.
Martianus Capella	4th–5th cent. A.D.
Nigidius Figulus	1st cent. B.C.
Nisus	1st cent. A.D.
Pliny the Elder	23 to 79 A.D.
Plutarch	c. 46 to 120 A.D.
Pompeius	5th cent. A.D.
Priscian	5th–6th cent. A.D.
Probus	4th cent. A.D.
Quintilian	c. 35 to 95 A.D.

Sacerdos	3rd–4th cent. A.D.
Sergius	4th–5th cent. A.D.
Servius	4th–5th cent. A.D.
Stilo (L. Aelius)	*c.* 154 to 90 B.C.
Terentianus Maurus	2nd cent. A.D.
Terentius Scaurus	2nd cent. A.D.
Varro	116 to 27 B.C.
Velius Longus	2nd cent. A.D.

APPENDIX B

The pronunciation of Latin in England

Anyone who has listened to Latin as pronounced until recently in the Westminster play, or at Grace by elder members of Oxford and Cambridge high tables, or in legal phraseology, will be aware that it bears little relation to the pronunciation of Latin with which we have been concerned. This 'traditional' English pronunciation was the result of a variety of influences.

In the first instance, Latin in England had from earliest times been affected by native speech-habits. Already in the Old English period vowel-length had ceased to be observed except in the penultimate syllable of polysyllabic words, where it made a difference to the position of the accent (hence correctly e.g. *mínǐma, minóra*). Otherwise new rhythmical laws were applied, the first syllable of a disyllabic word, for instance, being made heavy by lengthening the vowel if it were originally light (hence e.g. *pāter, lībrum, ōuis, hūmus*, for *pǎter*, etc.); there seems, however, to judge from Aelfric's grammar, to have been a practice of preserving Latin quantities in verse. 'Soft' *g* was pronounced as a semi-vowel [y], and intervocalic *s* was voiced to [z].

After the Norman conquest, Latin in England was taught through the medium of French, by French schoolmasters, and this resulted in the introduction of some peculiarities of the French pronunciation of Latin, e.g. the rendering of both consonantal *i* (*iustum*, etc.) and 'soft' *g* (*gentem*, etc.) as an affricate [dž] (as in English *judge*). 'Soft' *c* came to be pronounced as [s] (after the thirteenth century, when earlier French [ts] changed to [s]); all vowels were shortened before two or more consonants, e.g. in *census, nullus*; and Romance practice reinforced the tendency to lengthen vowels in open syllables (e.g. *tēnet, fōcus*, for *tĕnet, fŏcus*).

Not until the mid fourteenth century did English begin to

establish itself as the medium of instruction for Latin (owing largely to the efforts of the educational reformer John Cornwall). Thereafter Latin in England continued to develop along national lines, until the publication in 1528 of Erasmus' dialogue *De recta Latini Graecique sermonis pronuntiatione*, which comments on a number of national peculiarities in the current pronunciation of Latin and seeks to reform them in the direction of the classical language. The dialogue is written in a light-hearted style, and the disputants, in the manner of didactic fables, are represented in animal guise, as *Ursus* and *Leo*, the bear being the instructor. The dialogue makes a number of important deductions about the ancient pronunciation of Latin, including the 'hard' pronunciation of *c* and *g* before all vowels, the voicelessness of intervocalic *s*, and the importance of vowel length.

Erasmus made two visits to England, one to London in 1506 and another from 1509 to 1514. During his second visit he spent some time in Cambridge, and it was here that his views on Latin and Greek pronunciation were later most vigorously propagated. In 1540 John Cheke was appointed as the first Regius Professor of Greek in Cambridge, and his friend Thomas Smith, another classical scholar, as Regius Professor of Civil Law. Both were only twenty-six at the time, and had been deeply impressed by Erasmus' published work. Erasmus had limited himself to precept, and seems never actually to have used his reformed pronunciation; Ursus in fact comments that it is better to humour existing habits than to get oneself laughed at and misunderstood; in the words of Erasmus' predecessor in reform, Jerome Aleander, 'scientiam loquendi nobis reservantes, usum populo concedamus'.[1] Erasmus does, however, set the spoken word high amongst his educational priorities ('primum discet expedite sonare, deinde prompte legere, mox eleganter pingere'), and it is clear from the dialogue that he hoped for a gradual improvement in pronunciation.

In Cambridge, Cheke and Smith set about a radical and practical reform of both Greek and Latin pronunciation on Erasmian lines; Cheke in fact devoted six inaugural lectures to

[1] A clear echo of Cicero, *Or.*, 160 (see pp. 95 f.).

the subject, on successive days, under the title '*de literarum emendatiore sono*'. The reforms were, however, opposed by the Chancellor of the University, Stephen Gardiner, Bishop of Winchester, who in 1542 published an edict specifically forbidding the new pronunciation of either language. As penalties for infringement, M.A.s were to be expelled from the Senate, candidates were to be excluded from degrees, scholars to forfeit all privileges, and ordinary undergraduates to be chastised. For some time Gardiner's authority triumphed, but the intellectual weakness of his position is clear from some of his arguments; he complains, for example, that undergraduates are becoming insolent, by using an 'exotic' pronunciation, and delighting in the fact that their elders cannot understand it. He objects that the reforms would put Cambridge out of step with Oxford (and Oxford, as Gardiner elsewhere comments, 'liveth quietly')—to which Cheke replies, 'Neque tantum mihi quid Oxonia faciat, quam quid facere debeat, cogitandum. Neque minor est Cantabrigiae laus, si ipsa ad promovenda studia aliquid quaerat, quamquam Oxonia eadem retardet.'

Cheke later supported the claims of Lady Jane Grey, and briefly acted as her Secretary of State. Gardiner, who had spent most of Edward's reign in the Tower, was released on the accession of Mary, and made the most of his restored powers. Having earlier defended Henry's breach with Rome, he presided at the reconciliation under Mary, and preached at court, on the eve of Jane's execution, in favour of severer treatment for political offenders. Cheke's property was confiscated, and he was imprisoned in the Tower for more than a year. He was subsequently given leave to travel abroad and proceeded to Padua, and thence to Strasbourg, but was brought back to England only to die a broken man in 1557. On Elizabeth's accession the next year, Gardiner's edict was repealed (the Bishop himself having died in 1555).

But reformers had still to reckon with inertia and with the vested interests of the 'traditional' pronunciation of Latin; and in any case the advantages of the new pronunciation in England were soon to be diminished by an accident of linguistic history.

For the reforms came at a time when the extensive changes from the Middle English to Modern English vowel system were still incomplete; and so any reforms in Latin or Greek pronunciation underwent these vowel-changes as sub-dialects of English—the Latin vowels *ā*, *ī*, *ē*, for example, became diphthongs [ey], [ay], [iy], as in English *name, wine, seen*.

It was thus a strangely pronounced language, far removed from classical Latin, which was current in England by the nineteenth century. Apart from the peculiarities already discussed, the following features may be mentioned. In polysyllables with light penultimate, the antepenultimate (accented) vowel was, with some exceptions, shortened—hence e.g. *stāmina, sexagēsima* became *stămina, sexagĕsima*; *Oedipus* became *Ēdipus* and *Caesaris* became *Cĕsaris* (*oe* and *ae* being pronounced as *e*—hence also *Ēschylus* for *Aeschylus*): but, for example, verbal *amāveram, mīserat*. This shortening did not take place in the case of an *u* (hence e.g. *tūmulus* for *tŭmulus*, with lengthening), nor if there was hiatus between the last two syllables (hence e.g. *ālias, gēnius* for *ălias, gĕnius*, with lengthening: but compounds *ŏbeo, rĕcreo*, etc.). On the other hand, shortening took place in any case if the vowel was *i* or *y* (hence *fĭlius, Lȳdia*). The 'parasitic' *y*-sound which precedes an English *u* was treated as a consonant, and so *văcuum* remained '*văcyuum*' and did not become *vācuum*. The lengthening seen in e.g. *ītem* for *ĭtem* applied also to *mihi* (*mīhī*) but not, surprisingly, if the following consonant was *b* (hence *tĭbĭ, sĭbĭ, ĭbĭ, quĭbus*).[1]

Since English spelling is largely historical, the traditional pronunciation is of course often equivalent to a reading in terms of English spelling conventions—though it is not entirely so accounted for.

By the mid nineteenth century, however, schoolmasters were beginning at least to observe vowel-length in open syllables (doubtless owing to the exigencies of metrical teaching), and

---

[1] For these and further details see especially J. Sargeaunt, 'The pronunciation of English words derived from Latin', in *S.P.E. Tract* No. 4, and G. C. Moore-Smith, 'The English language and the "Restored" pronunciation of Latin', in *Grammatical Miscellany offered to O. Jespersen*, pp. 167 ff.

later the 'hard' *c* and *g* were being introduced in some quarters. Around 1870 a new reformed pronunciation of classical Latin was formulated by various Cambridge and Oxford scholars. The matter was discussed in that year by the Headmasters' Conference, but compromise resolutions by Oxford, together with some actual opposition, delayed the general introduction of the reforms; and it was only in the early twentieth century, under initiative from such bodies as the Cambridge Philological Society and the Classical Association, that the earlier prejudices began to be overcome in English schools and universities. Reaction, however, died hard, and even as late as 1939 *The Times* saw fit to suppress a letter against the old pronunciation by the Kennedy Professor of Latin at Cambridge.[1]

These reforms can hardly be said to constitute a thorough-going reconstruction of the classical pronunciation. They do not go so far as to involve any actually non-English sounds, or even English sounds in unfamiliar environments; and it is the bridging of the gap between the 'reformed' and a 'reconstructed' pronunciation that forms one of the purposes of this book.

The traditional English pronunciation was certainly far removed from classical Latin—but it was not the only offender amongst 'national' pronunciations. Latin in France had been pronounced along national lines from earliest times, with a particular disregard for vowel-length and accentuation; vowels + *m* were pronounced as nasalized vowels, with consequent changes of quality—hence, for example, in Merovingian times *cum* is found spelt as *con*. Reform of pronunciation was one of the tasks entrusted to Alcuin by Charlemagne, but this resulted only in the requirement that every letter should be given *some* pronunciation; in later centuries we still find e.g. *fidelium* rhymed with *Lyon*, and Erasmus (who considered the French pronunciation the worst of all) observes that the French pronounced *tempus* as '*tampus*'. *u* was regularly pronounced [ü] as in French; *qu* was pronounced as [k]; and even the mis-

---

[1] On the recent history of the reform movement see L. P. Wilkinson, *Golden Latin Artistry*, pp. 3 ff. On ecclesiastical pronunciation see F. Brittain, *Latin in Church* (Alcuin Club Tracts, 2nd rev. ed.).

spelling *ch* in *michi, nichil* (see p. 45) was pronounced as the [š] in French *champ*. In the sixteenth century we find punsters identifying e.g. *habitaculum* with French '*habit à cul long*',[1] to quote one of the less scabrous examples.

In the mid sixteenth century more serious attempts were made at reform in France, notably by Charles Estienne, who had studied Erasmus' work, and wrote a treatise *De recta Latini sermonis pronunciatione et scriptura*, for the instruction of his nephew, Henri. But in France, as in England, the forces of reaction were strong. We are told, for example, that around 1550, when the professors of the Collège de France attempted to introduce such reforms, they were opposed by the theologians of the Sorbonne—who even tried to deprive a priest of his benefice for using the new pronunciation (condemning it as a 'grammatical heresy'). This conflict centred particularly on the pronunciation of *qu*, one of the key-words in the dispute being *quamquam*; thus, according to one tradition, an academic scandal came to be known as a '*cancan*' (and thence any kind of scandalous performance). Later attempts at reform in France have been less successful than in England, and have had to reckon with such reactionary bodies as the 'Société des amis de la prononciation française du Latin'.

One gains some idea of the unacceptability of various national pronunciations in the sixteenth century from Erasmus, who describes in his *Dialogue* how speakers from various countries delivered addresses in Latin to the Emperor Maximilian. A Frenchman read his speech 'adeo Gallice' that some Italians present thought he was speaking in French; such was the laughter that the Frenchman broke off his speech in embarrassment, but even greater ridicule greeted the German accent of the next speaker; a Dane who followed 'sounded like a Scotsman', and next came a Zeelander—but, as Erasmus remarks, 'dejerasses neutrum loqui Latine'. Ursus here asks Leo, who tells the story, whether the emperor himself was able to refrain from laughter; and Leo assures him that he was, since 'assueverat huiusmodi fabulis'.

[1] Tabourot, *Bigarrures*, ch. 5 ('Des équivoques latins-françois').

Erasmus says that in his day the best speakers of Latin came from Rome, but that the English were considered by the Italians to be the next best. This statement is sometimes quoted with some satisfaction in England; but it should be noted that Erasmus significantly qualifies the claim by the words '*secundum ipsos*'. One has also to record the account given by another great Dutch scholar, Scaliger, at the beginning of the seventeenth century, regarding the Latin pronunciation of an English visitor: 'Anglorum vero etiam doctissimi tam prave Latina efferunt, ut...quum quidam ex ea gente per quadrantem horae integrum apud me verba fecisset, neque ego magis eum intelligerem, quam si Turcice loquutus fuisset, hominem rogaverim, ut excusatum me haberet, quod Anglice non bene intelligerem.' Such a performance can hardly be accounted for simply on the basis of the changes in the English vowel system between the sixteenth and seventeenth centuries.

Finally, it should perhaps be mentioned that the Italianate pronunciation of the Roman Catholic church, whilst it is probably less far removed from classical Latin than any other 'national' pronunciation, has no special status as evidence for reconstruction. An attempt to spread the Italianate pronunciation throughout the Catholic church was made in a letter of Pope Pius X to the Archbishop of Bourges in 1912, an attempt which met with some success after the First World War; at the present day this movement may be expected to be intensified as a result of the *Constitutio Apostolica de Latinitatis studio provehendo* ('Veterum sapientia', 22 Feb. 1962) of John XXIII. But it is of interest to note in this connexion an article by the Vice-Rector of the Biblical Institute in Rome (*L'Osservatore Romano*, 14 March 1962) which advocates 'a return to the pronunciation of the ancient Fathers of the Church' in the light of current linguistic research.

A note on the pronunciation of gn

In William Salesbury's treatise on Welsh Pronunciation (1567) there is the interesting observation: 'Neither do I meane here to cal them perfite and Latinelike Readers as many as do reade *angnus*...for *agnus, ingnis* for *ignis'*, which suggests that our reconstructed pronunciation of *gn* (see p. 23) had earlier antecedents in England. This pronunciation seems also once to have been traditional in German schools. E. J. Dobson (*English Pronunciation 1500–1700*, II, 1006 f.) suggests that the *ngn* pronunciation in England was based on the teaching of the Latin grammarians—but in fact they have nothing to say on the matter; and the arguments now used to reconstruct the pronunciation had not yet been proposed. We do, however, surprisingly find this pronuncation prescribed in Erasmus' *Dialogue*; his conclusions appear to arise partly out of an over-interpretation of Marius Victorinus (who in fact discusses *ng* but not *gn*), and partly out of an inadequate analysis of the Italian pronunciation of *gn*. He thus by chance arrived at the correct answer by entirely false reasoning; and his work could be responsible for the subsequent English and German pronunciations.

There remains a problem, however, in the apparent existence of yet earlier pronunciations of this type, at least in England. Somewhat before Erasmus' *Dialogue*, Skelton had rhymed *magnus* with *hange us*, though perhaps one should not attach much importance to this. As early as the fourteenth century one finds spellings with *ngn* for Latin-derived words, as *dingnete* in the *Ayenbite*; these could be based on the common Old French spelling, with the first *n* indicating nasalization of the preceding vowel—in the fourteenth-century *Tractatus Orthographiae* of Coyrefully, composed in England for the English, we read: '*g* autem posita in medio diccionis inter vocalem et consonantem habebit sonum quasi *n* et *g* ut *compaignon* (a phonetic misanalysis like that of Erasmus regarding Italian)....Tamen Gallici pro majori parte scribunt *n* in medio ut *compaingnon*... quod melius est.'

In English grammar schools up to at least the mid fourteenth century, French schoolmasters will have pronounced *gn* as a palatal [ñ]. English students may well have compromised with a pronunciation [ŋn], i.e. velar + dental nasal (the palatal being articulated midway between the two). They would be en-

couraged in this by the spelling of Latin-derived words borrowed through French (like *dingnete*), and by phonetic analyses
such as that of Coyrefully. The pronunciation of Latin *gn* as
[ŋn] in England could therefore have arisen well before Erasmus'
reconstruction.

SUMMARY OF
RECOMMENDED PRONUNCIATIONS

'English' refers throughout to the standard or 'received' pronunciation of southern British English.

		For discussion see page
ă	As first *a* in Italian *amare* (as vowel of English *cup*:[1] N.B. not as *cap*)	47 ff.
ā	As second *a* in Italian *amare* (as *a* in English *father*[1])	47 ff.
ae	As in English *high*	60 f.
au	As in English *how*	60 ff.
b	(1) As English *b*	21
	(2) Before *t* or *s*: as English *p*	21 f.
c	As English or French 'hard' *c*, or English *k*	14 f.
ch	As *c* in emphatic pronunciation of English *cat*	26 f.
d	As English or French *d* (on *ad-*, see p. 22)	20 f.
ĕ	As in English *pet*	47 ff.
ē	As in French *gai* or German *Beet*	47 ff.
ei	As in English *day*	63
eu	See p. 63.	
f	As English *f*	34 f.
g	(1) As English 'hard' *g*	22 f.
	(2) *gn*: as *ngn* in *hangnail*	23 ff.
h	As English *h*	43 ff.
ĭ	As in English *dip*	47 ff.
ī	As in English *deep*	47 ff.
i consonant	(1) As English *y*	37 f.
	(2) Between vowels: = [yy]	38 ff.
k	As English *k*	15

[1] Less accurate approximations.

III

SUMMARY OF RECOMMENDED PRONUNCIATIONS